THE
BEFUDDLED
STORK

THE

*Helping Persons
of Faith Debate
Beginning-of-Life Issues*

BEFUDDLED
STORK

Edited by
Sally B. Geis &
Donald E. Messer

ABINGDON PRESS/Nashville

THE BEFUDDLED STORK
HELPING PERSONS OF FAITH DEBATE BEGINNING-OF-LIFE ISSUES

Copyright © 2000 by Abingdon Press

This book is printed on recycled, acid-free, elemental-chlorine–free paper.

Library of Congress Cataloging-in-Publication Data

The befuddled stork: helping persons of faith debate beginning-of-life issues/edited by Sally B. Geis & Donald E. Messer.
    p. cm.
Includes bibliographical references and index.
ISBN 0-687-08925-5 (alk. paper)
    1. Human reproductive technology—Moral and ethical aspects. 2. Abortion—Moral and ethical aspects. 3. Human reproductive technology—Religious aspects—Christianity. 4. Human reproductive technology—Religious aspects—Judaism. 5. Abortion—Religious aspects—Christianity. 6. Abortion—Religious aspects—Judaism. I. Geis, Sally B., 1928– II. Messer, Donald E.

RG133.5 .B437 2000
176—dc21

                                     99-086137

The editors owe a profound debt of gratitude to Fredrick R. Abrams, M.D., for his creative imagery of "the befuddled stork," which he graciously allowed us to use as the title of this book.

02 03 04 05 06 07 08 09—10 9 8 7 6 5 4 3 2

MANUFACTURED IN THE UNITED STATES OF AMERICA

To

Don's grandchildren—

Rachel Christine and Noah Christopher Gallagher

and

Sally's son and daughter-in-law

James P. Geis and Beverly J. Walter

CONTENTS

ACKNOWLEDGMENTS

Writing a trilogy of books that explore complex contemporary issues requires both a special friendship between coeditors, and the assistance of a host of very special friends to whom we are deeply indebted. This book, along with *Caught in the Crossfire: Helping Christians Debate Homosexuality* and *How Shall We Die? Helping Christians Debate Assisted Suicide*, has only been possible because of unique connections that have crossed the traditional boundaries that unfortunately often separate persons of faith.

We were not totally surprised to read former president Jimmy Carter's report of how trying to write the book *Everything to Gain* with his wife, Rosalynn, almost broke up their forty-year marriage! Unfortunately, we do not have Rosalynn's account, but we can imagine that she found him to be equally stubborn and difficult. Carter recounts:

> It was amazing to find how differently we remembered the important events of our lives together, and how differently we reacted to them. As the writing progressed, we couldn't speak to each other about the book, and could communicate only by writing vituperative notes back and forth on our word processors. Rosalynn treated my portions of the text only as rough drafts, but hers as having been carved in stone, just come down from Mount Sinai! Finally, our editor suggested that the more controversial paragraphs be allotted to just one of us, and identified in the final text with either a "J" or an "R." We'll never be coauthors again![1]

Fortunately, the two of us have found the coediting task to involve a minimum of conflict and a maximum of compatibility. Bonding the coeditors through the course of a multitude of editing disagreements and decisions has been a very positive and caring personal and professional relationship. We have brought to this series of volumes distinct perspectives and experiences, yet we have always been able to blend these differences, because we share a common spirit and seek to discover a life-centered ethic and theology.

Critical to this and other volumes has been the gracious cooperation of persons who share dramatically different viewpoints from ours. Especially important have been the contributions of more evangelical Protestant and Catholic writers and consultants, who have helped us ensure that these three volumes reflected a truly ecumenical breadth of opinion and reflective judgment. Illustrative are the authors in this manuscript. We want to express our deepest gratitude to each of them: Fredrick R. Abrams, M.D.; Peter J. Paris; R. Albert Mohler, Jr.; Ronald Cole-Turner; Marilyn E. Coors; Ruth L. Fuller, M.D.; Judith Craig; Sidney Callahan; Judy C. Martz; Harvey C. Martz; Stanley Hauerwas; Joel Shuman; Tex S. Sample; Joan Burgess Winfrey; Lee M. Silver; Gerald L. Zelizer; and Abigail Rian Evans.

Behind this distinguished assembly of authors stands an incredible circle of consultants who have enabled us to complete this manuscript. With deep appreciation, we acknowledge the assistance of Delwin Brown, Lisa Cahill, Cynthia Cohen, Virginia Culver, Mary Catherine Dean, Jessica Edwards, Marshall Eidson, Christine Gallagher, J. Raymond Geis, Margaret Hoeppner, Jennifer Kanouse, H. John Kilner, Mary Stewart van Leeuwen, Joretta Marshall, Alice Matthews, Vinh T. Pan, David Petersen, Maura A. Ryan, Elizabeth Stephen, Allen D. Verhey, Beverly Walter, Timothy Weber, Sondra Wheeler, Dana Wilbanks, and J. Philip Wogaman. Of course, none of the persons mentioned in these acknowledgments bear any responsibility for the final text.

Special words of gratefulness must be extended to Suzanne Calvin and Fredrick R. Abrams, who repeatedly served as professional advisors; to Alberta L. Smith, who expertly helped compile and type these essays; and to the Iliff School of Theology for its generous support of scholarship. Above all, without the encouragement and understanding of our beloved spouses, Robert B. Geis and Bonnie J. Messer, these volumes certainly could never have been produced.

We hope and pray that this trilogy of books will help persons of faith, Jewish and Christian, as they struggle with questions of life as varied as sexual orientation, death and dying, infertility, in vitro fertilization, abortion, genetic engineering, and cloning. Our purpose has never been to tell others how to think, but to help all of us to reflect theologically and ethically about these challenging quandaries of life. May this trilogy not only strengthen one's own opinions, but also provide windows of understanding on why other conscientious persons think differently.

NOTE

1. Jimmy Carter, "President, Peacemaker, Poet," *The Washington Post National Weekly Edition,* July 17-23, 1995, p. 29. *Everything to Gain: Making the Most of the Rest of Your Life* was published in 1995 by the University of Arkansas Press.

CONTRIBUTORS

Fredrick R. Abrams, M.D., is director of the Clinical Ethics Consultation Group, associate clinical professor of Obstetrics and Gynecology at the University of Colorado Health Sciences Center, and associate medical director of the Colorado Foundation for Medical Care. He is past chairman of the National Ethics Committee of the American College of Obstetricians and Gynecologists and was appointed to the National Advisory Board on Ethics and Reproduction. He founded the Center for Applied Biomedical Ethics at Rose Medical Center in Denver, Colorado, the first center for the study of ethical issues in a community hospital setting.

Sidney Callahan is author of nine books as well as a multitude of essays, columns, and articles. Her work has appeared in a wide variety of publications, including the *Hastings Center Report, Soundings, Commonweal, Theological Studies, Psychology Today, Los Angeles Times, Newsday, and The New Republic*. She has served as a columnist for *Health Progress*, the official journal of the Catholic Health Association of the United States, and *Commonweal* magazine. She has lectured at more than three hundred colleges and appeared on numerous television programs, including the *Today Show*, the *MacNeil/Lehrer NewsHour,* and William Buckley's *Firing Line*.

Ronald Cole-Turner is H. Parker Sharp professor of theology and ethics at Pittsburgh Theological Seminary, and an ordained minister in the United Church of Christ. He is a member of the Program Dialogue on Science, Ethics, and Religion of the American Association for the

13

Advancement of Science, and a member of the Dialogue Project on Human Germ Line Modification. He also chairs the Task Force on Genetic Engineering, United Church of Christ. He is the author of numerous papers and books on religion and science, including his recently acclaimed *Human Cloning: Religious Responses.*

Marilyn E. Coors is a postdoctoral fellow at the University of Colorado Health Sciences Center in the Departments of Ethics and Human Genetics. A Roman Catholic laywoman, she holds advanced degrees in both genetics and ethics. She serves on various ethics committees and boards, including Denver Children's Hospital Ethics Committee, and the boards of Regis University and the Seeds of Hope Charitable Trust, which funds education for inner-city children from impoverished families. She has also served as director of the Bio-Ethics Project for the American Academy for the Advancement of Core Curriculum.

Judith Craig was elected a bishop in The United Methodist Church in 1984. She received a master of divinity degree from Union Theological Seminary in New York, and a master of religious education degree from Eden Theological Seminary in Missouri. She serves on numerous boards of her denomination as well as within ecumenical organizations. Previously assigned to oversee the Michigan Area, she currently serves the Ohio West Area of The United Methodist Church. Her essay, "A Bishop's Letter to Her Goddaughter," appeared in *Confessing Conscience: Churched Women on Abortion* (Abingdon Press, 1990).

Abigail Rian Evans is associate professor of practical theology, and academic coordinator of field education at Princeton Theological Seminary. She holds a doctor of philosophy degree from Georgetown University and a master of divinity degree from Princeton. Her interests focus on bioethics, pastoral care, health ministries, vocation and ministry, and spiritual formation. Her work is interdisciplinary and church oriented. Her denominational affiliation is Presbyterian Church, U.S.A.

Ruth L. Fuller, M.D., is associate professor of psychiatry at the University of Colorado Health Sciences Center. Prior to her appointment in Colorado, she served as director of a mental health clinic in East Harlem and was in private practice in Harlem, New York. Her many consulting appointments have included the Sickle Cell Center at Children's Hospital and the Child Protection Team at University Hospital in Denver. She also serves as mentor to minority medical students. Her published works focus primarily on women and children in cross-cultural and minority settings. She is an elder in the Presbyterian Church, U.S.A.

Sally B. Geis was the founding director of the Iliff Institute for Lay and Clergy Education. She is an associate clinical professor of psychiatry at the University of Colorado Health Sciences Center. Her articles on grief, AIDS, and interracial communication appear primarily in medical journals, including *Hospice Journal, Journal of Diseases of Children*, and *Journal of Family Practice*. She is author of one and coeditor of two books on frequently debated subjects within the religious community, namely homosexuality and assisted suicide.

Stanley M. Hauerwas is the Gilbert T. Rowe professor of theological ethics at the Divinity School, Duke University. A prolific author, Hauerwas is ordained in The United Methodist Church. Among his books are *Unleashing the Scripture: Freeing the Bible from Captivity to America; After*

Christendom: How the Church Is to Behave If Freedom, Justice, and a Christian Nation Are Bad; and (with William H. Willimon) *Resident Aliens: Life in the Christian Colony.* A well-known teacher, author, seminary speaker, and cultural critic, he has contributed many essays on medical ethics, including "Abortion, Theologically Understood" in *The Church and Abortion: In Search of New Ground for Response* (edited by Paul T. Stallsworth).

Harvey C. Martz is senior minister at St. Andrew United Methodist Church in Littleton, Colorado. He holds a doctor of ministry degree from the Iliff School of Theology, and received the school's Alumnus of the Year Award in Parish Ministry in 1996. His master of divinity degree is from Perkins School of Theology, Southern Methodist University. His articles have appeared in *Circuit Rider, Net Results,* and *United Methodists Today.* He also writes guest editorials for the *Denver Post.*

Judy C. Martz is cofounder and served for fourteen years as codirector of PEAK Parent Center, a Colorado statewide advocacy organization for families and educators of children with disabilities of all kinds. She holds a master of arts degree from the University of Colorado at Colorado Springs and a bachelor of arts degree from Midwestern State University in Wichita Falls, Texas. She has conducted training seminars throughout Colorado and the nation. She and her husband have two children: a twenty-six-year-old son who has Down syndrome, and a daughter who is a junior in college.

Donald E. Messer has been president and Henry White Warren professor of practical theology at the Iliff School of Theology since 1981. Included among his nine books are *Contemporary Images of Christian Ministry; A Conspiracy of Goodness; Christian Ethics and Political Action;* and *Calling*

Church and Seminary into the 21st Century. With Sally B. Geis, he has coauthored *Caught in the Crossfire: Helping Christians Debate Homosexuality* and *How Shall We Die? Helping Christians Debate Assisted Suicide.* An elected member of The United Methodist General Conference and World Methodist Council, he is listed in "Who's Who in America."

R. Albert Mohler, Jr. is president and professor of Christian theology at the Southern Baptist Theological Seminary. He is an ordained minister and has been the editor of the *Christian Index,* a publication of the Southern Baptist Convention. He has contributed chapters to several recent books, including *Here We Stand: A Call from Confessing Evangelicals* and *The Coming Evangelical Crisis.* He is editor-in-chief of the *Southern Baptist Journal of Theology.* He hosts *The Bible and Life,* a weekly television program. He is listed in "Who's Who in America." In 1998, *Change,* a national higher education magazine, named him one of forty "Young Leaders of the Academy."

Peter J. Paris is Elmer G. Homrighausen professor of Christian social ethics at Princeton Theological Seminary, and liaison with the Princeton University Afro-American Studies Program. He is ordained in the African United Baptist Association. His publications include three books as well as many book chapters and articles. He serves on the editorial board of several journals, including the *Journal of Religious Ethics* and *Journal of the American Academy of Religion.* Paris is past president of the Society of Christian Ethics and the American Academy of Religion.

Tex S. Sample was the Robert B. and Kathleen Rogers professor of church and society at St. Paul School of Theology. Known as a working-class theologian, Sample focuses on the social analysis of contemporary church life. Recent published works include *U.S. Lifestyles and Mainline Churches; Hard Living People and Mainstream Christians; White Soul: Country Music, the Church and Working Americans; The Spectacle of Worship in a Wired World.* An ordained United Methodist clergy, he holds his Ph.D. degree from Boston University in Christian Social Ethics and Sociology of Religion.

Joel J. Shuman is visiting lecturer in Theological Ethics at the Divinity School, Duke University. Shuman holds a bachelor of science degree from the Medical College of Virginia and serves as a physical therapy consultant and clinician. He holds a doctor of philosophy degree from Duke University, where he received the Kenan Dissertation Fellowship. He was awarded a grant in long-term care and chronic illness research from the Duke Medical School. His published works include his forthcoming book, *The Body of Compassion: Medicine, Ethics, and the Church,* and numerous articles.

Lee M. Silver is a professor at Princeton University in the departments of Molecular Biology, Ecology, and Evolutionary Biology, and the Program in Neuroscience. He is also associated with the Program in Science, Technology, and Environmental Policy at Princeton's Woodrow Wilson School of Public and International Affairs. Silver is coeditor-in-chief, together with Ian Wilmut, of a new international journal entitled *Cloning: Science and Policy.* His book *Remaking Eden: Cloning and Beyond in a Brave New World* has led to appearances on radio and television in Asia and Europe, as well as in Canada and the United States.

Joan Burgess Winfrey is associate professor of counseling at Denver Seminary. Prior to her appointment at Denver Seminary, she was a professor in the School of Education

18

at Metro State College. She holds a doctor of philosophy degree in clinical psychology and special education from the University of Denver, and a master of arts in special education, with emphasis on learning disabilities and emotional disturbance, from Adams State College in Alamosa, Colorado. She is a licensed psychologist with a psychotherapy practice specialized in grief, transition and loss, and women's issues.

Gerald L. Zelizer has been rabbi of Congregation Neve Shalom in Metuchen, New Jersey, since 1970. A fourth-generation rabbi, he served as president of the International Rabbinical Assembly from 1992–94. He is currently a member of the Committee on Jewish Law and Standards, which formulates religious policy for the Conservative Movement. He is on the Board of Contributors of *USA Today,* and has also published in the *New York Times, Los Angeles Times,* and *Chicago Tribune.* Prior to his arrival in Metuchen, he served as rabbi of a congregation in Buenos Aires, Argentina.

INTRODUCTION

FACING ETHICAL DILEMMAS: ANCIENT AND MODERN

Sally B. Geis

T he day after our five-year-old son started kinder-garten, he developed an excruciating headache and a high fever. By morning we knew he had encephalitis. We did not know how this swelling of his brain would affect his physical and mental abil-ities. We would need to wait—how long no one could say. One day, during the first nine months of our son's bed rest, I sensed that time was dragging as badly for him as it was for me. So I said too brightly, "Jimmy, would you like to play a game?" He thought a minute and then replied, "I don't think so. Right now I don't feel brave enough to lose."

This book is for the many persons facing difficult deci-sions about conceiving and bearing children and who are not sure they are brave enough to take a chance on los-ing. Should they play the "games" new technology makes possible or should they not?

Dilemmas of Infertility and Reproduction

For most people the question may seem irrelevant. For them procreation is easy, the most natural thing in the world. But ponder the couples who want desperately to have children but have trouble conceiving. In 1995, 6.2 million women in the U.S. reported that they had experi-enced infertility—that is 1 out of every 10 women aged fifteen to forty-four.[1] Should any of these persons take the financial and medical risks involved in the use of assisted reproductive technology? Is it morally permissible to do so?

Think of the parents whose badly malformed baby lived only a few hours. Should they try again? If they do conceive again, should they seek information about possible defects in the maturing fetus? If the potential infant has serious defects, should the parents abort the fetus? What does God want them to do?[2]

What of the young girl raped by her mother's boyfriend? How brave does she feel? What risks shall she take? Will she consider abortion? Should she tell her mother? consult a doctor? talk with a rabbi, priest, or minister?

Finally, we look toward emerging questions that must be answered in the not-too-distant future. What of cloning and genetic engineering that alter the genetic characteristics of babies yet to be born? Should we, as a people, condone such research? Suppose a couple is told, through genetic counseling, that their baby is at risk for inheriting a fatal disease? If genetic technology could eliminate the disease from the baby's genes, should the couple consent to the procedure? Or suppose that cloning could produce bone marrow badly needed by a living child? If cloning were possible, should the parents consent in order to save the existing child?

A growing number of women and men of faith face these questions. This book is for them, their children, their extended families, their communities of faith, and their clergy.

New Technology Requires Fresh Ethical Thinking

Medical technology is altering the circumstances surrounding birth. Therefore theologians, ethicists, pastoral counselors, faithful laypersons, and the public at large are called to reassess and renew their theological and ethical understanding of these mysterious moments of entry into human existence here on earth.

Currently, neither religious scholars nor the public at large are in agreement about what it means to "do the right thing" in these situations. In *How Shall We Die? Helping Christians Debate Assisted Suicide,* we addressed the differences of opinion that have developed in the religious community as technology changed the meaning of death by learning how to keep some patients alive almost indefinitely.[3] We offered careful analyses from thoughtful, well-informed ethicists and theologians who came to differing conclusions. We did so believing that, given a well-balanced discussion, our readers, in community with other faithful persons, are capable of discerning for themselves what it means to die well.

Perhaps it is unrealistic to hope that theological consensus can ever be reached on matters as complex as reproductive dilemmas. However, we dare to hope that a careful consideration of divergent ethical points of view will make each of us more understanding of others who may have different experiences and a dissimilar point of view. It may also help us examine our own reasoning and develop better conclusions.

We believe that nascent theological discussion about assisted reproductive technology and cloning will soon develop into strident debates reminiscent of those surrounding assisted suicide. Therefore, in the same spirit as was embodied in our assisted suicide book, we offer this publication.

Entering a Brave New World with Ancient Foundations

Making babies is the only means by which humanity perpetuates itself from one generation to the next. No other human activity is as fundamental to our surviving as a species. No wonder it is sometimes described as *the* essential human yearning.

Throughout most of history, human procreation took place by means of a single process—male-female copulation. Given its importance, it is no surprise that since ancient times persons have sought to control procreation. Surrogate parenthood did not emerge in contemporary culture, nor did concern about pregnancies considered as mistakes or violations of God's will.

As humanity faces complex new moral, ethical, and theological dilemmas created by new scientific developments, we may find comfort in knowing that our foremothers and forefathers in the faith faced similar dilemmas related to reproduction. Their efforts to control procreation were often fraught with anxiety and unintended consequences, just as are our contemporary efforts.

Biblical Struggles with Infertility and Procreation

The Bible contains numerous stories about our spiritual forebears' struggles with infertility, and their efforts to produce heirs, including the use of surrogates (Genesis 16). It also contains at least one story that could be interpreted as a description of God's intervention in order to terminate a pregnancy (Numbers 5)!

These accounts speak of the grief as well as the joy that a pregnancy, or lack of one, can evoke. Consider the story of Sarah, desperate to provide an heir for Abraham, arranging for Hagar to act as her surrogate. The unpredicted results of that decision sound hauntingly modern (Genesis 16). Hagar's hatred toward Sarah after she, Hagar, conceived and bore a son by Abraham rings in our ears as we read of the current, bitter legal battles fought over babies created through the use of egg donors or sperm donors with whom legal contracts have been made by persons eager to have a child of their own.

Sometimes persons involved in the use of these sophisticated techniques become angry and disenchanted with one another.[4] Donors sometimes have second thoughts about giving up the children they produce. Parents under contract have been known to change their minds and reject babies.

Sarah and Hagar are not the only women of the Hebrew Bible to suffer anxiety, bitterness, and envy over giving birth and over being barren. Remember Hannah, who "wept and would not eat" even though her husband said to her, "Hannah, why do you weep? Why do you not eat? Why is your heart sad? Am I not more to you than ten sons?" (1 Samuel 1:7-8). In this story, as in the story of Sarah, God shows mercy and compassion for a barren woman by answering Hannah's prayer for a son. Samuel is born and given to the Lord (1 Samuel 1:13-19).

Think also of Leah and Rachel (Genesis 30). Though Leah bore Jacob four sons, she still did not curry his favor. Who can judge that Rachel's anxiety over her barrenness was more poignant than Leah's distress over the results of her efforts to please? So it is today. Social workers and family counselors have ample evidence that pregnancy does not make lonely young women better loved, nor unstable marriages more idyllic. Frequently the opposite occurs, as new parental responsibilities and problems present themselves.

Terminating pregnancy is also discussed in the Bible. For example, Numbers 5 illustrates the ancient response of husband, God, and community to a wife's presumed infidelity (Numbers 5:11-31). If a husband suspects his wife is pregnant by another man, he may take her to the temple where the priest will give her "the water of bitterness that brings the curse."

"If no man has lain with you, and if you have not turned aside to uncleanness while under your husband's authority, be immune to this water . . . that brings the curse. But if you have gone astray . . . the Lord make you an execration. . . ." (Numbers 5:19-21)

Apparently, God acting in judgment may create an induced abortion, freeing family and community from this unclean pregnancy. (For further theological commentary on this passage, see Tex Sample's discussion in chapter 7 of this volume.)

Contemporary obstetricians speculate that the "water of bitterness" was probably ergot, which has a bitter taste and causes vasoconstriction and muscle constriction. Even today it is occasionally used postpartum (after childbirth) to constrict the uterus if excessive bleeding occurs.

Contemporary Infertility Treatments

Rachel's lament, "Give me children, or I shall die" (Genesis 30:1), is a modern plea as well as an ancient one. Infertile couples today spend thousands of dollars and submit to humiliating and dangerous procedures in an effort to produce their own offspring, often with disappointing results. The cost varies, depending on the procedure used and the number of times it is used. For example, in vitro fertilization costs $8,000 to $10,000 a month. The cost per successful outcome ranges from $66,667 (for the first cycle) to $114,486 (for a couple in their sixth cycle).[5]

Facts about the success rate are almost as surprising as the cost figures. A Centers for Disease Control study, conducted in 1995, reports that only 24 percent of the cases in which assisted reproductive technology was used resulted in clinical pregnancy. Furthermore, nearly a quarter of these clinical pregnancies did not result in live births.[6]

This age-old urge to control the beginning of human life is enhanced by ever-expanding scientific knowledge and technology in microbiology and genetics. Some say the new knowledge, and the technology it has created, can and will revolutionize the means of human reproduction. Though most children in today's world are still created "the old-fashioned way," there is an increasing number being created with the assistance of enhanced fertilization technology. Hardly a week goes by that we do not learn from the media about a circumstance in which persons are using new fertilization technology in some newsworthy manner. One couple recently received publicity for advertising their willingness to pay $50,000 to an egg donor of a certain height and IQ.[7] Another couple came into the spotlight for producing eight babies at once after fertilization treatment. For those of us who watch these developments from the sidelines the implications are mind-boggling!

In Vitro Fertilization Dilemmas

Some believe the technology of in vitro fertilization is so evil that it should not be allowed. Yet for many families who do make use of in vitro fertilization the abortion question has been complicated by ethical dilemmas related to the destruction of embryos (fertilized eggs). These dilemmas are a product of the *in vitro* process itself, the process of creating potential embryos to implant in a womb. Frequently several embryos, perhaps as many as nine, are produced at the same time. The medical justification for the production of so many is that the process is both expensive and difficult. Therefore, it makes sense to use as many eggs and sperm as are available, in order to ensure that even one embryo will be produced and successfully transplanted into a uterus.

The medical explanation seems straightforward

enough, but what about the moral and ethical implications? When does life, as defined by theologians, begin? Theologians and ethicists, as well as the public, argue heatedly over these questions and often disagree in extreme ways.

Think now of the couple who are informed that they have produced seven, eight, or nine embryos that may potentially become fully formed babies. These potential parents must decide what to do in light of their theological understanding of life. They will do so in a highly polarized cultural environment where their decision is apt to be debated publicly within the media and from the pulpit.

For some persons of faith such a dilemma does not pose an ethical problem. They rely on obstetricians who believe the human uterus was not designed to carry "litters," as are the uteri of some other mammals. They know from experience that the effort to carry a large number of fetuses at once often results in premature births and tiny babies. Underweight babies run the risk of suffering blindness, motor impairment, and a variety of significant and complex problems. These couples may, in good conscience, have some of the embryos frozen before implantation for possible use at another time; or after implantation, some embryos can be destroyed *in utero* for the protecting and salvaging of the remainder.

However, some persons have reached other theological and ethical conclusions. They view the embryos as "gifts from God." Not implanting all of them would be immoral, no matter how much inconvenience or risk they pose to the mother.[8] These persons trust God to solve any problems that may arise—and problems are a possibility. A month after octuplets were born, one of the physicians in the neonatal intensive care unit where the babies were placed was quoted as having said, "There is still a 10 percent or so risk of some long-term problems, but I hope we are not going to see anything like blindness, deafness, mental retardation, or severe cerebral palsy."[9]

The myriad of physical, legal, and moral implications of in vitro fertilization led to the creation of a National Advisory Board on Ethics in Reproduction (NABER) in 1991. The board was asked "to step into a vacuum in American public life created by the lack of a national body to initiate and stimulate debate about ethical and policy issues arising in reproductive practice and research."[10]

Medical ethicist Cynthia Cohen introduces her summary of the ethical conclusions of the board by reminding readers that human reproduction has always evoked powerful emotions as well as social conventions. In our highly diverse society, with its pluralistic views on values, the board concluded that at a minimum these values should guide reproductive choices: (1) respect for personal autonomy, (2) support of individual and family privacy, (3) promotion of the well-being of participants, (4) concern for the interests and welfare of children, (5) acknowledgment of the requirements of professional ethics, (6) recognition of basic values that tie us together as a community, and (7) awareness that the process of creating life is relational in nature. Special priority and concern must be given to assuring that those relationships created by methods of assisted reproduction are protected and flourish.

The summary also emphasizes the board's concerns for "basic values important to our life as a community, such as non-commodification of human beings and their bodies, the moral significance of the family as a basic social unit, equal respect and concern for all human beings, and the fair and appropriate distribution of societal resources."[11]

Ultimately, the board plans to develop a comprehensive ethical framework that can be used to guide the development of current and future reproductive technologies that is grounded in careful case studies of several reproductive technologies.

The religious community should study the report of the commission and then contribute to the societal debate about the ethics of in vitro fertilization, and the public policies that should be developed related to it.

Abortion and Defining Consciousness

Why discuss abortion in a book about creating life? Abortion does not assist in the creation of new life. On the contrary, abortion seeks to prevent it. In this country, the disagreement about abortions of any kind has become so violent that legal abortion clinics are picketed and in some cases vandalized. Physicians willing to perform abortions are harassed and even murdered because some persons believe the physicians are "baby killers." Be clear, no one writing in this volume comes from an extremist position that would advocate such violence. We hope their measured differences of opinion will be helpful to couples who live in the climate of extremism and are forced to make difficult decisions.

The topic of abortion is included because we believe that new scientific knowledge has complicated the abortion debate by creating situations not previously encountered. While a scientific understanding of the beginning of life may affect ethical thinking about difficult abortion decisions, one's theological understanding of life's beginning may well have more influence on these new situations than science.

Another technological development that brings psychological confusion that may influence theological thinking about potential life is the ultrasound. Ultrasound images show the physical development of the fetus in such a graphic way that many laypersons take the images as "scientific proof" that these developing embryos are real people. People believe that "if it looks like a baby, it is a baby." The assumption is confirmed by obstetricians who report that families frequently bond to the ultrasound image. To think otherwise is counterintuitive and runs against common sense. My own personal experience falls into this category.

Our older son, who is a radiologist, arrived one day while I was caring for his two-year-old, my granddaughter. Without saying a word he went to the VCR, put in a tape, and pushed "play." What we saw was a developing fetus in a womb. I was enthralled. I could see the little fingers and toes moving right before my eyes. My granddaughter glanced at the pictures and said, "See Didi, that's our baby swimming." She was right.

She had been with her parents when her daddy took those pictures of her mommy's tummy, so she knew all about the image. What she did not understand was that pictures like these are taken to monitor the normality of a developing fetus. These graphic images, contrary to our common-sense belief, do not tell us when consciousness occurs.

Psychiatrist Ruth Fuller and microbiologist Lee Silver, who introduce two sections of this book, offer two different kinds of scientific definitions for the beginning of life, one psychosocial and the other biological. Silver points out that it is impossible to know exactly when consciousness arises. And it can arise at different times in different situations. For example, anacephalic babies (born with no brains) are not "conscious," even though they may have gestated for nine months.

Fuller speaks of the psychological complexity of defining consciousness or the beginning of life. She believes the potential mother's definition of the situation is both important and real. It will affect the mother's future life and the future of the potential infant. A woman who has been raped may not perceive the unwelcome changes in her body as a baby. She may define it as a hideous growth created out of violence and violation. Fuller believes that this woman's perception of what is happening within her is as real as an obstetrician's diagnosis of her pregnancy as the development of a fetus. We err if we believe a moral society can treat this rape victim as if she were in the same situation as a woman who yearns for a baby to be part of her loving family.

Some theologians rely heavily on these scientific perspectives; others do not. Whatever conclusion one reaches, it is wise for us to be informed by each of these perspectives. If the religious community displays ignorance and disinterest in new developments in reproductive technology, it does so at its own peril. Good scientific information will not eradicate differences of opinion. However, if we are to be credible to the society at large, we must do better than to simply retreat into polarized liberal and conservative positions based on scanty information, or worse yet, on scientific assumptions that are simply wrong.

On the Horizon: Genetic Research and Cloning

Human cloning was not a possibility in biblical times, and is not yet a reality in our time. However, research in molecular biology, genetics, and reproduction is yielding results heretofore known only as science fiction. When Ian Wilmut announced the cloning of "Dolly" the sheep in February 1997, his announcement dominated the news media for weeks.[12] Of course it was not the cloning of a sheep that concerned the public. It was the thought that soon humans might be cloned, too. Ninety percent of Americans polled within the first week after the story broke felt that human cloning should be banned.[13]

As those of us in the Jewish and Christian traditions

assimilate this knowledge, we hear again the ancient words in Genesis spoken by the serpent who urged Eve to eat the fruit that would give her knowledge: "You will not die; for God knows that when you eat of it your eyes will be opened, and you will be like God, knowing good and evil" (Genesis 3:4-5).

The new issues that cloning and other advances in molecular biology and genetics present seem so significant for the new millennium that a section of this book is devoted to the theological and ethical questions involved. We do so because we agree with Philip Boyle, president of the Park Ridge Center for the Study of Faith, Health, and Ethics, who fears that the Jewish and Christian traditions will be left in the dust as decisions are made in the political arena.[14]

His concerns echo Rabbi A. James Rubin, who believes that religious authorities—including ministers, rabbis, and priests—must understand the new circumstances and become involved in ethical decision making in new ways and in new places. Ethical questions once discussed as abstractions within churches and synagogues are now being faced in research laboratories, hospitals, and court rooms. If the religious community does not soon become deeply involved in this bioethical decision-making milieu, the decisions will be made solely by others, such as lawyers, legislators, research scientists, and physicians. It will be an immense moral tragedy if religion is "cut out of the process."[15]

Rethinking Responses to Cloning

Governments and many religious groups reacted negatively to the news of Dolly. The British government responded to Wilmut's achievement by withdrawing his research funding. The Congress of the United States banned the use of federal funding for all work on human embryonic stem cells. Scientists in embryology and genetics responded with dismay. They point out that the effect of the ban will be to terminate the work of university professors, who depend on federal funding and who are held accountable to approved scientific standards. The ban affects not only work related to cloning, but also work with embryonic stem cells that "may have real potential for treating such devastating illnesses as cancer, heart disease, diabetes, and Parkinson's disease."[16] Any work done now will be in the private sector, where the motivation is most apt to be financial reward and the controls are few.

Two weeks after the Dolly announcement, *The United Methodist Reporter* ran this headline: "Is Dolly a Lamb of God or Forbidden Science?" The article reported that the Vatican had called for an outright ban on all human cloning and urged scientists not to genetically alter any animal species. Southern Baptist and United Methodist leaders in the United States also called for a ban.

However, other religious thinkers resist the idea of automatically outlawing new genetic discoveries. Instead, they suggest a moratorium on cloning experiments until scientists and ethicists can sort out the issues. Lutheran theologian Ted Peters was quoted as saying, "[I am] not in favor of wildcat cloning, nor do I think it should be banned forever and ever." The real nightmare scenarios, in Peters' view, would be intentional or unintentional genetic damage done by private reproductive technology clinics that would sell cloning services.[17]

Ethicist Karen Lebacqz points out that most theologians are asking whether cloning destroys human uniqueness.[18] Does a clone have individuality? personality? identity? a soul? Theologians who believe cloning should be banned conjure up the *Boys from Brazil* scenario, suggesting that clones can become an evil force like Hitler's army. Theologians who believe cloning is not evil accept the identical-twin analogy, that clones are indeed individual persons.

Both answers address the wrong question, according to Lebacqz, who contends that a "soul is something that happens between God and people. . . . It is not an individual possession but a statement about relationship. Soul has to do with our relationship before God. Would a human clone have a soul? Of course."[19]

Lebacqz's deep concerns about cloning are the same as her concerns about in vitro fertilization. They are justice concerns. She asks, *Where are women's voices?* "Cloning takes an egg, a womb, and the care and nurture of a newborn. . . . Human eggs come from women. Human wombs are found in women."[20] But when a major conference on cloning was announced for June 1997, the program did not include a single woman as a major speaker.

These subjects are too new and too vast to be covered thoroughly in our book about making babies. However, it is deemed important, at least, to introduce the issues and hint at the theological and ethical concerns they evoke, including questions about justice.

Facilitating Informed Thinking and Decision Making

Our goal in presenting these essays is to help persons of faith think more clearly about the issues, not to tell them what to think. The book is about human quandaries that cause deeply felt and often urgent anxieties. Many who must make decisions about procreation face constraining time limits. Postponing decisions too long can result in losing some opportunities forever.

This book does not treat the decisions as abstract ethical concerns that can be understood or solved through theoretical discussion. We agree with Silver, that "before one can speak rationally about the origin of a human being, it is critical to gain a feel for the biology of embryonic and fetal development, between fertilization and birth." However, "the agenda will not be set by scientists.

. . . the agenda is sure to be set by individuals and couples who will act on behalf of themselves and their children."[21] Neither will the agenda be established by theologians or church dictates, even though both science and theology may inform people's decisions.

As coeditors, we are not without opinions, principles, and convictions, nor are we monolithic in our beliefs. However, our goal is not to impose our beliefs on others, but rather to expose readers to various convictions so that they can reach reflective theological and ethical judgments on their own.

Complex problems have complex solutions. We believe that dogmatic, inflexible pronouncements are not particularly helpful to persons involved in making decisions presented by reproductive dilemmas.[22] Solutions must take into account the wide variety of specific circumstances in which decision makers find themselves. No simple answer fits all situations. This is why our chapters have the titles that they do, and why we asked more than one author to address each issue. The titles describe authentic problems faced by sincere and honest people. The two essayists for each chapter were chosen because they have training and experience in understanding ethical principles, but reach different conclusions about the moral appropriateness of the decision to be made in the situation. The dissonance is intentional. We call on readers to weigh the evidence in light of real human dilemmas and to make up their own minds.

An Organizational Overview

A short introduction, written by a physician/scientist who works with reproductive concerns, opens each of the three parts of this book: reproductive technology, abortion, and cloning. The purpose of these introductory sections is twofold: (1) to help those of us who are not well versed in obstetrics, molecular biology, and genetics to better understand the basic scientific facts of reproduction in our present highly complex technological world; and (2) to explain not only the scientific complexity of the issues but also the human predicaments they present in the lives of real people. Readers may also refer to the glossary, provided at the end of the book, for definitions of scientific words used within the text.

Each chapter consists of two commentaries by knowledgeable persons who reach different conclusions about the morality of the particular situation. The authors range from academic theologians to lay activists. An editor's overview sets the stage for each question to be debated. The conclusion proposes some guidelines for those who seek to be loyal to their faith while making decisions about difficult questions related to human reproduction. Our question is: If we or our families and loved ones were faced with these situations, how should we respond?

The intended audience is primarily laypersons of Christian or Jewish faith and secondarily public policy makers. The omission of other religious perspectives is not intended to indicate that other views are not valid. Space limitation was the deciding factor. Length also constrained a full discussion of particular medical circumstances. For example, some readers might wish for an in-depth discussion of certain genetic anomalies such as Tay-Sachs. Others might wish for more information about certain assisted fertilization techniques. We wish that more medical information could have been included. However, our focus is on the theological and ethical dilemmas created by new knowledge and technology. Examples within the book are illustrative of the circumstances in which these dilemmas take place. They are not comprehensive discussions of medical conditions.

Should We Play These Technological Games?

At the beginning of this chapter, I posed a question: Do we feel brave enough to tamper with human reproduction and face the consequences, intended and unintended? The urge to control procreation is an ancient one, but are we willing to risk the consequences? Some authors within this book warn of dire potential dangers in the use of technology, particularly for cloning and/or genetic alteration. Others argue against all tampering with nature. They argue against abortion and in vitro fertilization as well.

Each reader will need to reach conclusions on these matters grounded in her or his theological beliefs and understandings of emerging scientific information. All of us will be influenced by past experience as well as present circumstances. I know that I am.

The idea of creating this book about God's plan for babies occurred to me one Sunday as I participated in a postbaptism ritual used by my local church. After the clergyperson baptizes a baby, the cleric carries the baby up and down the aisles of the church so that we, the people who make up the baby's community of faith, may see, close-up, this person whom we have promised to nurture within the faith. During this time, the congregation sings Ronald Cole-Turner's lovely hymn, "Child of Blessing, Child of Promise."

> Child of love, our love's expression,
> Love's creation, loved indeed!
> Fresh from God, refresh our spirits,
> Into joy and laughter lead.[23]

Often during this symbolic walk the baby, wide-eyed and bewildered, looks expectantly at us, the people in the pews. How shall persons of faith respond to this expectant gaze?

Surely, in spite of our differences of opinion on issues discussed in this book, we know full well how God wants each of us to treat all babies, regardless of how they were made.

We are called to be in loving community with all mothers, fathers, and children, potential and actual. We are to treat them with love and respect, whether or not we agree with the decisions they reach about questions posed in these pages.

Does God care how we make babies? Of course. Surely God is with those of us making decisions about something so important as a new life. Furthermore, we know that human decision making about procreation will never be perfect. We will make some mistakes, no matter how hard we try to do the right thing. But we can take comfort in remembering that God walks with us through risks, dilemmas, difficulties, and even mistakes, perceived or real. And we know that all babies, no matter how they were conceived and nurtured, come to us "fresh from God."

NOTES

1. Anjani Chandra and Elizabeth Hervey Stephen, "Impaired Fecundity in the United States: 1982–1995," presented at the annual meeting of the Population Association of America, Washington, D.C., 29 March 1997.

2. For an excellent discussion of these ethical questions see Rebekah Miles, "Knitting Life in the Womb," *Christian Social Action* (October 1998): 13-15.

3. See *How Shall We Die? Helping Christians Debate Assisted Suicide*, Sally B. Geis and Donald E. Messer, eds. (Nashville: Abingdon Press, 1997).

4. See Fredrick R. Abrams, "The Befuddled Stork," unpublished paper delivered to the Colorado Medical Society, Vail, Colorado, 15 May 1999.

5. Elizabeth Hervey Stephen, "America's Most Wanted Children: The Social Context of Infertility," a paper read at the 1998 Annual Meeting of the Population Association of America, Chicago, Illinois, 13 April 1998, p. 4.

6. CDC on-line Reproductive Health, 1995 National Report: Section 2. Access *http://www.cdc.gov/nccdphp/drh/arts/ fig8b.htm./.*

7. Susan Estrich, "Egg Money," a syndicated column that appeared in the *Denver Post*, 8 March, 1999, sec. B, p. 7.

8. "Mom Slept Upside Down to Prolong Pregnancy: 8 Tiny Babies Continue Fight for Survival," an Associated Press story that appeared in the *Denver Post*, 22 December, 1998, sec. A, p. 6.

9. Lawrence K. Altman, "Surviving Octuplets Are Gaining on Life." A *New York Times* story reprinted in the *Denver Post*, 7 January 1999, sec. A, p. 2.

10. *New Ways of Making Babies: The Case of Egg Donation*, Cynthia B. Cohen, ed. Commissioned by the National Advisory Board on Ethics and Reproduction (NABER) (Bloomington and Indianapolis: Indiana University Press, 1996).

11. Ibid., pp. 245-46.

12. K. H. S. Campbell et al., "Sheep Cloned by Nuclear Transfer from a Cultured Cell Line," *Nature* 380 (1996): 64-66.

13. Lee Silver, *Remaking Eden: How Genetic Engineering and Cloning Will Transform the American Family* (New York: Avon Books, 1998), pp. 105-7.

14. Joan Connell, "Is Dolly a Lamb of God or Forbidden Science?" *The United Methodist Reporter,* 14 March, 1997, p. 2.

15. A. James Rubin, "Clergy Aren't Prepared for Moral Dilemmas in the Hospital Room," *The United Methodist Reporter,* 19 April 1996, p. 4.

16. Nicholas Wade, "Cow-Human Cells 'Trouble' Clinton." A *New York Times* story reprinted in the *Denver Post*, 15 November 1998, sec. A, p. 3.

17. Ibid.

18. Karen Lebacqz is the Robert Gordon Sproul professor of theological ethics at Pacific School of Religion in Berkeley, California.

19. Karen Lebacqz, "Cloning: Asking the Right Questions," *Ethics and Policy*, a publication of the Center of Ethics and Social Policy, Graduate Theological Union (Winter 1997): 4.

20. Ibid.

21. Silver, *Remaking Eden*, pp. 10-11, 48.

22. Robin K. Sterns, "Double or Nothing," *Santa Clara Magazine* (Autumn 1997): 10. In this discussion of the ethics of human cloning, Sterns describes the work of the Markkula Center for Applied Ethics at Santa Clara University, a Jesuit school, stresses the complexity of the issues surrounding decisions about cloning. Scholars at the center are reluctant to make absolutistic pronouncements about cloning.

23. Used with the written permission of Ronald Cole-Turner, 1999.

PART ONE

QUANDARIES OF CONQUERING INFERTILITY

CHAPTER ONE

THE BEFUDDLED STORK

Fredrick R. Abrams, M.D.

lthough *avoiding* procreation from coitus dates back at least to the Old Testament, the first attempt to *accomplish* procreation without sexual intercourse was reported in 1878. William Pancoast, a professor at Jefferson Medical College in Philadelphia, used the semen of one of his medical students to impregnate a woman whose husband had been found to be infertile.[1] The pregnancy that resulted from this sperm-donor artificial insemination was disclosed when the offspring turned twenty-five. It was denounced as contrary to the laws of God, and as "mechanical rape."

A century later, in England, Patrick Steptoe took the method a step further with in vitro fertilization. The process involved mixing egg and sperm in a glass dish (*in vitro* = in glass), a few days of incubation in a nurturing medium, and the implantation of the eight-cell embryo into the uterus of the mother-to-be. Soon after came an announcement from Australia of the first frozen-embryo pregnancy, showing that the fertilized egg could be preserved by freezing, then implanted with no ill effects. More recently, the egg alone has been frozen, thawed, and fertilized successfully. The physiological components of reproduction have been separated into (1) egg suppliers, (2) sperm suppliers, (3) womb suppliers, and (4) where and how gametes are joined.

After millennia of knowing exactly what was meant by

the words *mother, father,* and *child,* various assemblages of the four listed components have made the words ambiguous. Selected sperm, eggs, and uteri have since been joined to make embryos, with the possibility of having three different mothers (an egg supplier, a womb for rent, and a mother to rear the child), and two fathers (the sperm supplier and the rearing father). There are sixteen possible combinations, plus the newest variant—cloning. After centuries without a change in her job description, is it any wonder that the stork is befuddled?

Whether these innovations to relieve the anguish of persons who can reproduce no other way will be a positive or negative influence on values believed important to human coexistence remains to be seen.

Unprecedented Dilemmas

Society continues to try to deal with truly unprecedented dilemmas that accompany this technology. When ethical strangers (persons who do not share the same values) are in conflict, they turn to the law, which we all share. One advantage of media coverage of these conflicts is exposure of dilemmas that may thereafter be avoided by advance planning. Situations that have arisen include: (1) disposition and/or custody of frozen embryos after death or divorce of the genetic parents; (2) custody and/or responsibility for a newborn whose surrogate mother (egg and womb provider) did not wish to relinquish the child to the (contracting) genetic father at birth, or contrarily, a newborn whose contracting parents did not want to accept or provide for the child; and (3) responsibility for a newborn genetically unrelated to either the rearing (contracting) parents or the gestational mother. When there was a contract about disposition of frozen embryos, courts in California and New York have upheld the agreement. A Massachusetts court did not. But if doctors and patients would insist on clarifying these issues and reaching a decision before proceeding, many times courts might be avoided.

Breaking up reproduction into its component parts separates actions from responsibility. Deliberate confounding of the genetic parent-child relationship certainly changes the original meaning of parenthood. Society is confused because the basis in courts for awarding custody varies, sometimes depending on genetics, sometimes on gestation, sometimes on a business contract. Some courts have ignored relationships and settled disputes based on which parents they believe serve the best interests of the child.

Asking the Right Questions

The ideal users of in vitro fertilization are married couples with blocked tubes. They overcome a physical barrier and have a conventional pregnancy with the "right" genetics and a happily-ever-after outcome. Essential to pursuing these practices is true and thoroughly informed consent. That includes hazards that the patients, in their eagerness to parent, may never have considered. It is the responsibility of the doctor to raise issues patients never thought of. Patients do not know what questions to ask.

First, let's consider questions important to donors. Few donors consider they ought to have any responsibility toward the new life that they may have a role in creating. Egg donors may fantasize that their egg will be used to make the lives of a happily married couple complete. Few to none of the gamete donors have been told of the possibilities of their gametes being used outside of the idealized couple. Right or wrong, donors may choose not to donate to single parents or to same-sex partners. What about anonymity? Are donors willing to be known to the prospective parents and their offspring? And if doctors use those that are unwilling to be identified, donors need to be warned that their role might be discovered, either by law or by the appalling lack of confidentiality in medical record keeping.

The surgical and hormonal interventions that donors must go through are the same processes for women who are going to provide their own eggs for the procedure. Donors as well as prospective parents must be told of the specific physical hazards of the surgery involved, and of the side effects of the intense hormone stimulus to force ovulation. But the psychological factors, especially for donors, are no less important. They should be advised to consider their future feelings when they have their own children—or worse, if they are unable to have children. Of course, all of this information may discourage donation or the use of this technology by fearful prospective mothers. Although that is not the goal of the doctor on behalf of the infertile patients, it is the ethical obligation of the physician who is admonished in the first place to "do no harm." Doctors truly interested in informing will have much of this material written out for careful consideration by prospective patients, and insist they take sufficient time to review it all.

The Dangers of Multiple Pregnancies

The discussion of multiple pregnancies must be thoroughly explored. Women born with their full supply of eggs who do not ovulate are being treated with hormones, but it isn't without technical and ethical fallout. Multiple pregnancies threaten patients' health and safety. After leading patients into this dilemma, we offer another difficult moral choice: aborting some of the fetuses. This option is one some patients can't take because of their earnestly held convictions about the status of a fetus. The possibility of selective termination must be settled before embryo transfer is undertaken. If embryos are transferred, the number should be limited. Recent research with successful implantation of fewer embryos may offer a way out of this problem. But there can be trouble even when no transfers are involved. The recent septuplets came from an egg "explosion" from the mother's ovaries overstimulated by hormones. Ultrasound could reveal that too many eggs are available, and intercourse could be avoided or contraception used for that cycle to avoid creation of a "litter."

Many infertility patients have such an intense desire to create a child that they forget this process is not over with pregnancy and delivery. These babies become children and adults. Their origins become important to them. Considerations such as donor anonymity must be settled initially. If donors are family members, both donor and recipient ought to be made aware of the difficulties that arise as the children grow. New family tensions result from the atypical relationships, with disagreements about how children should be raised. If either the father or mother is genetically unrelated to the child, the couple must explore what effect their asymmetrical relation to the child may have on their marriage.

There is much cultural pressure to forge ahead ignoring the hazards. Prospective parents owe it to themselves, their partners, and the hoped-for child to be thoroughly informed, even though the hazards, once known, may mitigate against using these techniques.

NOTE

1. Gena Corea, *The Mother Machine* (New York: Harper & Row, 1985).

CHAPTER TWO

IS IT MORAL TO MAKE "TEST-TUBE BABIES"?

Overview

For centuries procreation was by way of sexual intercourse. Now the mythical "stork is befuddled," notes Fredrick R. Abrams, M.D., as a plethora of innovative ways of making babies presents new biological options and unique ethical dilemmas.

Artificial insemination and in vitro fertilization (so-called "test-tube babies") particularly present a host of medical, legal, theological, and moral questions. Separating reproduction into components separates actions from responsibility and deliberately confuses genetic parent-child relationships. Also, the possibilities and dangers of multiple pregnancies emerge frequently.

Peter J. Paris and Albert R. Mohler, Jr., respond differently to the query, Is it moral to make "test-tube babies"? Paris endorses in vitro fertilization as a positive for infertile couples because it poses only "minimal moral threats." As long as in vitro fertilization (IVF) is "conjoined with and not a substitute for mutual love," it fulfills the human yearning for parenthood. Paris addresses the issues of mini-abortions, selective reductions, distributive justice, genetic manipulations, ova and sperm banks, and potential threats to the family. He basically believes that most of the ethical dilemmas can be overcome by ensuring that "love alone is the primary requisite for excellence in child care and the well-being of the family as a whole." Loving caretakers, be they gay, lesbian, or heterosexual, will serve the good of a child. Caring nurture, during gestation and after birth, are more important than IVF.

Mohler denounces in vitro fertilization and procreative liberty as compromising human dignity and contravening the natural limits God has set. Babies should be "begotten, not merely made"; children are not technological products, but "gifts of a loving God" to married heterosexual couples. IVF contributes to a "godless world" by weakening marital bonds, challenging the integrity of the family, introducing a third person into a marital relationship, and permitting unmarried women, homosexuals, and lesbians to become parents. Frozen embryos and the use of embryos in medical research threaten the sanctity of life. Selective reduction procedures mean that "the abortion culture hangs over the IVF laboratory." Mohler believes Christians should avoid IVF and oppose its use.

IS IT MORAL TO MAKE "TEST-TUBE BABIES"?

A *Response by* Peter J. Paris

It is a curious fact that most of the ethical issues in modern medicine were made possible by the extraordinary progress of late twentieth-century biological science and technology. In fact, many of them were hardly imaginable a generation ago. As with all human knowledge, progress in one sphere of life often raises moral dilemmas when new cultural possibilities are seen as realizable. Their emerging presence invariably threatens both the established ways of life and the moral ethos that attend them. Clearly, different possibilities pose greater or lesser moral threats to either the social order or its spiritual foundation. In this essay, I will argue that only minimal moral threats attend the procedure that science has named "in vitro fertilization" and which the general public often calls "test-tube babies."

A More Advanced Form of Artificial Insemination

IVF is a more advanced form of artificial insemination. While the latter procedure involves the use of a syringe to deposit sperm in the uterus of a woman during her time of ovulation, IVF entails three steps: namely, the surgical removal of the ova from the woman, their fertilization in vitro, and their implantation in the uterus. The ova and the sperm may or may not be provided by the husband or wife. Not infrequently either the ova or the sperm is provided by a donor, and surrogate mothers are sometimes used.

As technological aids for procreation, both methods have

brought fulfillment to many couples who were greatly troubled by their inability to procreate apart from such assistance. Since the capacity to procreate is given by nature, those who are unable to do so, for whatever reason, often experience an overwhelming sense of inadequacy due in large part to familial and societal expectations. Because of their strong desire to procreate they have welcomed these advances in biological technology as their means to personal fulfillment. The first baby in the United States born by means of IVF occurred in 1981. Today, both IVF and artificial insemination are almost commonplace throughout the country. Yet, they do present ethical problems and moral concerns for many. In fact, the Roman Catholic Church officially opposes both, largely on the grounds that they are believed to be contrary to God's design for procreation. In contrast to that position, I contend that the artificiality of the process cannot in itself be a sufficient reason for declaring the procedure immoral. Such reasoning would require the elimination of much of modern medicine and the entire field of biological technology. We must not forget that such medical techniques as kidney dialysis, respirators, blood transfusions, and organ transplants are all artificial interventions that few people oppose for ethical reasons.

An Expression of Mutual Love

Now ethics is the art of reasoning about morality. While the normative criteria for it vary, they inevitably reflect both the moral ethos and the prevailing religious values of the particular society in which the reasoning occurs. In my judgment, the purpose of ethics is to enhance the quality of human action by enabling people to actualize their full potentialities. Since every form of knowledge, including science and technology, expresses the human capacity to understand the human condition, the many and varied advances in biological science and technology have contributed to the well-being of humanity in countless ways, not the least of which are these artificial means of procreation. Clearly, knowledge may serve either good or bad ends. Insofar as IVF is used to help men and women exercise their capacity for procreation, and insofar as it is conjoined with and not a substitute for mutual love, it contributes to the good of all concerned, as countless testimonies by the parents of so-called "test-tube babies" have attested.

The Issues of Mini-Abortions and Selective Reductions

Those who view the origin of human life as occurring at the moment when an ovum is fertilized object to the process of IVF because it often involves hyperovulation so as to fertilize many ova in the attempt to ensure effective implantation of the embryo. Such persons view the process of discarding fertilized ova as mini-abortions, which they consider to be immoral. Most fail to notice, however, that countless numbers of so-called mini-abortions occur repeatedly in the natural process of becoming pregnant. Thus, on the one hand, I see little difference between the natural and artificial loss of such embryos. On the other hand, I concur with the judgment that human life cannot be considered apart from the embryo's viability outside the womb.

Thus, my thinking on the matter is similar to the compromise represented in the *Roe v. Wade* decision, where the well-being of women and the protection of fetal rights are balanced. More specifically, the right of the woman to choose was given priority up to the end of the first trimester, which marks the point of viability. Thereafter, the state's rights for protecting fetal development would assume its rightful place in decision making during the second and third trimesters.[1] Contrary to the mistaken opinions of most, *Roe v. Wade* did not grant women the right to have abortions on demand. Rather, significant limits were placed on that right.

Recently much media attention has been devoted to the birth of octuplets by a Nigerian woman in the United States who had undergone IVF. That event became the occasion for widespread discussion by doctors, ethicists, and others about the ethical concerns associated with such multiple births. The many and varied ethical concerns include the enormous cost of hospital care for such underdeveloped babies; the longtime medical care that will certainly be needed in the future; the likelihood of various kinds of physical and mental disabilities resulting from the babies' lack of fetal development; the strain on the mother's health; to say nothing of the ethics of overpopulation. In my judgment, all of these problems can be resolved by the process of selective reduction of embryos at the earliest possible period. Further, I contend that there is no ethical justification for allowing such a multiplicity of embryos to remain in gestation. In all such situations, selective reduction is the only good that can be justified.

A Matter of Justice

Unfortunately, most private insurance companies refuse to pay for IVF procedures, thus rendering the service accessible only to those who have the capacity to pay for it. Such an economic divide excludes large numbers of people, both in the United States and around the world, from sharing in its benefits. In fact, knowledge of such measures is virtually unknown in most cultures of the world where both men and women undergo much suffering and pain as a result of not being able to procreate. For example, in most African cultures marriage, apart from procreation, is viewed as unfulfilled, because children are often revered as the gateway between the historical and ancestral worlds. In fact, among many cultures people are excluded from the ancestral world by their failure to procreate, due to the necessary role that progeny must play in preserving the reciprocal relationships between the family and its ancestors.

Clearly, a more equitable system of distributive justice would relieve the suffering of countless numbers of people if they had access to IVF. While the problems in this country, for which IVF provides a solution, are limited to individual couples, they permeate whole communities in many other cultural contexts. Those who do not have the problem are prone to advise those who do to adopt children. While adopting children may well be a solution for some, and while it is a noble thing to do, it does not always suffice.

Addressing Other Ethical Concerns

Other ethical concerns arise whenever IVF is coupled with the scientific procedures of genetic manipulation. As with all things, differing moral weights attend differing genetic procedures. I think most people would welcome the effective alternation of a genetic structure destined to subject the child to some dreaded disease or disability. By contrast, most are prone to look askance at the problem of positive eugenics, preferential breeding of superior genotypes. Few are prepared to offer any guidance in this area. I find this strange, since selective breeding has been so commonplace among the breeders of livestock and pets. Might not the knowledge gained from those experiences help our thinking about its application to humans? I think we should engage in that discussion since the knowledge is at hand and will inevitably seek the means for its demonstration.

Another ethical concern pertains to that of ova and sperm banks and the many moral and legal issues that attend their presence. I think that these problems are more legal than moral. Some people abhor the idea that the frozen ovum or sperm of a dead person should be productive of a baby. I do not see a problem as long as the procedure is rooted in the love to nurture a child. If it be for some other reason, then one can rightly raise moral doubt, since the product of IVF is a person and not a thing. Persons are sacred beings created in the image of God and intended to contribute to the well-being of God's entire creation. Their capacities for doing so can be either enhanced or diminished by the quality of their nurture and care. How they came into the world is not as important as the context of love from which the invitation to life had been issued and into which they have been welcomed from the moment of birth onwards.

Love Alone Determines Family Excellence and Child Care

Finally, many people fear that such technical methods as IVF might signal a major threat to the nature of the family as we have known it. More specifically, they abhor the prospect that single men and women who do not desire marriage, and/or gay and lesbian partners might choose to have children by that means. Since I think that a child's healthy development is best enabled by the loving nurture of both male and female caregivers, the lack of either can hinder a child's development. Yet, that lack can be overcome by the subsidiary roles of loving surrogates who may be relatives or friends.

Most important, however, love alone is the primary requisite for excellence in child care and the well-being of the family as a whole. Since love always implies justice, which is the good of the other, none need to fear that the good of the child will be served by loving caretakers, whether they be gay, lesbian, or heterosexual on the one hand, or partners in same-sex or heterosexual marriages on the other hand. Further, how one comes to be is not as important as how one is nurtured during gestation and follow-

ing birth. Both are rightly societal concerns that are no
more threatened today by artificial means of procreation
than they were in previous generations. Appropriate societal regulations have always been required and must continue to be. But love is the primary theological and moral
virtue, the absence of which is wholly destructive not only
to human life, but also to the whole of God's creation.

NOTE

1. For a detailed ethical discussion of this entire matter, see Beverly
Wildung Harrison, *Our Right to Choose: Toward a New Ethic of Abortion*
(Boston: Beacon Press, 1983), pp. 31ff.

IS IT MORAL TO MAKE "TEST-TUBE BABIES"?

A Response by R. Albert Mohler, Jr.

Questions of human reproduction inevitably define what it means to be human, and the moral issues that arise in connection with sex and reproduction are among the most divisive controversies of our time. The development of "test-tube baby" technologies presents us with moral issues that demand answers and require our most careful thought and reflection.

German theologian Helmut Thielicke once argued that we learn more about ourselves and our most fundamental convictions by considering those "borderline" questions which resist easy answers. This is certainly true in the case of the new reproductive technologies. My purpose is to argue against the moral acceptability of in vitro fertilization. This argument cannot be understood apart from the foundational issues of human dignity, the meaning of personhood, and the integrity of marriage and the family.

Assisted Reproduction and the New World of Baby Making

The reproductive revolution is upon us. The past half-century has seen the development of reproductive technologies previous generations could not even imagine, much less consider in moral perspective. These technologies have radically expanded human control over the biological process, and have been designed both to prevent and to achieve successful pregnancy. Some legal theorists now argue for a new human right—the right to complete "procreative liberty," ensuring an individual's right to these new technologies.

The technological basics of in vitro fertilization are easy to understand. The moral issues are far more complex. *In vitro* literally means "in glass," for the actual fertilization of the egg takes place in a glass laboratory dish rather than in the woman's reproductive system. While infants conceived by this method are often called "test-tube babies," this is a misnomer, as no test tube is generally used. The phrase does, however, underline the technological character of the conception that takes place in the laboratory.

The moral issues are more complex. What does it mean to separate conception from the act of sexual union? To whom should these technologies be made available? What is the moral status of the fertilized embryos? Those who dismiss these questions as irrelevant or inconsequential show disrespect for human dignity and human life.

At one level, the moral and theological issues at stake in IVF are identical to those related to artificial insemination. The insemination may be done with sperm from the husband in a married couple (homologous insemination) or with sperm from a donor (heterologous insemination). Beyond this, a new set of issues emerge. In IVF, an egg is removed from a woman and is fertilized in a laboratory setting by the insertion of sperm cells into a dish. Once the egg is fertilized and the exchange of chromosomal material takes place, the embryo is implanted in the uterus, with the hope that implantation will occur and a pregnancy will continue to healthy birth.

Due to the high cost of each implantation and IVF sequence, multiple eggs are usually fertilized, and some embryos are implanted, with the remaining embryos kept frozen for possible future use. This practice often leads to multiple pregnancies, and in some cases healthy implanted embryos are then removed from the womb and destroyed—a process known as "selective reduction." IVF technologies were developed as a means of assisting married couples unable to achieve successful pregnancy through natural means. The technologies are now widely available, however, and some clinics direct and advertise their services especially to single women and lesbian couples. Both heterosexual couples and homosexual male partners have opted to "have" children by use of IVF with a surrogate "mother" hired to carry the baby to term.

Clearly, these practices and technologies raise the most fundamental questions about what it means to be human, and about God's intention for marriage and the family.

Manufactured Babies and the End of Parenthood

In the first place, human dignity is compromised by the artificiality of the IVF technology. The absolute separation of conjugal union and the sex act from the process of conception creates a new and artificial process of human reproduction—one that demands technological intervention at virtually every stage, from the collection of the sperm and eggs, to the actual fertilization, to the implantation of the embryo in the uterus.

This puts human agents in control of human destiny in a manner that overthrows natural limits. Theologians have debated this issue with intensity. Karl Rahner, the most influential Roman Catholic theologian of the century, believed that "there is really nothing possible for man that he ought not to do."[2] On the other hand, Protestantism's Karl Barth warned that this would lead to a "dreadful, godless world," one he could foresee in Aldous Huxley's *Brave New World*.

Clearly, God has placed natural limits upon our creaturely power and authority. Humans seem intent upon exceeding those limits in every sphere, and the rapid developments in biotechnology threaten to transform the understanding of what it means to be human. As Barth argued, human identity has been inherently related to parenthood and the conjugal bond.[3] What does it mean to think of humanity severed from this parental relatedness?

The new technologies of IVF underline the extent to which the modern mind has reduced human reproduction to a technology rather than a divine gift, mystery, and stewardship.[4] As Oliver O'Donovan argues, the biblical language reminds us that we are begotten, not merely made.[5] This is not a semantic irrelevancy. Our language betrays our understanding of the meaning of human procreation.

Children are not the products of a technological process, like common consumer commodities, but are the gifts of a loving God whose intention it is that children should be born to a man and a woman united in the bond of marriage, and, as the fruit of that marital bond, realized in the conjugal act. They are neither by-products of the sex act nor mere "products" of our technological innovations.

Paul Ramsey warned that we would be "de-biologizing" the human race by using these technologies. While we sympathize with couples unable to achieve conception by means within natural limits, these limits remain. "We ought rather to live with charity amid the limits of a biological and historical existence which God created for the good and simple reason that, for all its corruption, it is now—and for the temporal future will be—the good realm in which man and his welfare are to be found and served."[6]

Ramsey's warning against the "messianic positivism" of these new technologies is a corrective to those who believe that this is merely a Catholic concern. Protestants, too, have historically recognized the intrinsic relatedness of parenthood to the conjugal bond, and the act of marital sex as the design of a loving and merciful Creator who imposed limits for our good. IVF technologies threaten those limits in others ways as well. The IVF revolution has opened unprecedented opportunities for eugenics and the genetic manipulation of the embryo. Experiments on human embryos now involve the transfer of genetic material and offer the potential for genetic manipulation both before and after fertilization.

The technologies of IVF compromise the marital bond and threaten the integrity of the family. The use of donor sperm is unacceptable, for it brings a third party into the marital bond. The same is true for the use of a donor egg. A married couple should not invite the biological contribution of a third party—known or unknown. While the fertilization of the egg occurs in a laboratory (thus avoiding adultery), the marital bond is compromised by the use of another man's sperm or another woman's egg.

Beyond this, the use of IVF to allow unmarried women and lesbian couples to achieve pregnancy outside marriage and heterosexual relatedness is a direct rejection of God's intention in the creation of humanity as male and female, and the limitation of sexual relatedness to a man and a woman united within the marital covenant. IVF is welcomed by radical feminists and lesbian activists as a technological marvel that promises freedom from male involvement, except as sperm donors.[7] This is one specter of the "godless world" against which Barth warned.

The link between IVF and surrogacy is also deeply problematic. This allows a woman (or a couple) freedom from the burden and joys of pregnancy, but it also severs the maternal bond and reduces parenthood to genetic contribution. Again, the use of surrogates in connection with IVF by homosexual males (singles or couples) violates both the conjugal bond and the integrity of the family as the basis for parenthood.

The Status of the Embryos

The usual practice in IVF calls for the fertilization of numerous embryos, which are then frozen until needed for implantation in the womb. Though several embryos are implanted in most procedures, several embryos generally remain frozen and in a state of biological suspension. This may be the most devastating moral reality of IVF. These embryos—fully human in chromosomal development—are treated as human "seedlings." Sometimes euphemistically called "Embryo Eskimos," these embryos are denied human dignity and are reduced to a frozen existence, awaiting either implantation, indefinite storage, or willful destruction. In recent years thousands of human embryos have been destroyed in Great Britain, as they were no longer needed for implantation. The argument for this destruction was couched in " humane" language, implying that it is better to be destroyed than indefinitely frozen.

How does a couple (or an individual) deal with the knowledge that their genetic offspring are suspended in a state of frozen nonexistence? This horrible knowledge is a reminder of the violation of limitations, which always promises great gain but comes at a great (and even greater) cost.

The legal status of the embryos is now the subject of legal actions and judicial determination. In the case of a divorce, who "owns" the embryos? When a genetic "parent" dies, who inherits the embryos? The case of Steven and Maureen Kass illustrates the dilemma. Five fertilized embryos remain after the couple's divorce. Now, Maureen wants to have the embryos implanted and wants to raise the children. Steven does not want to have children, especially with his former wife, and wants to donate the embryos to medical research. A New York judge ruled for Maureen, declaring that fertilized embryos were the possession of the woman. An appellate court ruled that both "parents" must give consent to implantation.[8] Other cases are pending across the nation.

These questions underline another problem with the IVF technologies. It is now possible for an embryo to be implanted years after fertilization, opening the opportunity for a woman to give birth to her aunt, or even the genetic sibling of her grandmother. For that matter, an embryo can be implanted in a woman of advanced years, pushing the limits of reproductive capacity. Do we adjust our understanding of family and generational transfer to this new reality? This further undermines the integrity of the family and God's order of creation.

Finally, the use of embryos in medical research brings a new threat to the sanctity of human life. Restrictions on experimentation with embryos are progressively lifted, with some arguing that the thousands of "unused" frozen embryos represent an invaluable resource for biomedical experimentation and genetic research. This is hauntingly reminiscent of Nazi medical research. These embryos are human life worthy of full legal and ethical protection.

Selective Reduction: Murder in the Womb

The embryos "produced" by IVF face danger in the womb as well as in the laboratory. Multiple implantations—done for the sake of maximum effectiveness and minimum financial cost—lead regularly to multiple pregnancies. As with the use of fertility drugs, these multiple pregnancies can result in the fertilization and implantation of several embryos.

The reality of "selective reduction" came to the attention of most Americans through the media coverage of the McCaughey septuplets in 1997. Doctors and medical ethicists debated the morality of allowing so many fetuses to remain in the womb and progress toward full development. Many doctors argued for the moral imperative of selective reduction, which means the removal and destruction of selected embryos or fetuses.

Ezekiel J. Emanuel, chairman of the department of clinical bioethics at the National Institutes of Health, explained that "many people believe couples who agree to infertility treatments must not only be informed about, but also must consent to the potential need for selective reduction even before beginning the treatments."[9]

This abhorrent argument reveals the casual disrespect in which the embryo is held by so many people who are ready and willing to destroy innocent life in the name of life-giving technology. IVF technologies destroy even as they claim to create, and the termination and disposal of human embryos is a reminder that the gruesome reality of the Third Reich is never far from us. A society that will destroy human life and discard unwanted frozen embryos has lost the vital sense of human dignity that is foundational to civilized society. A culture comfortable with the knowledge that fetuses are destroyed in the name of life can rationalize itself into arguments identifying some humans—born and unborn—as "life unworthy of life." The abortion culture hangs over the IVF laboratory.

The Test Tube and the Test of Moral Judgment

In early 1999, advertisements offering $50,000 for an egg donor appeared in newspapers of the Ivy League schools and other leading national universities. The ads stipulated that the donor must be a healthy woman who had scored at least 1400 on the Scholastic Aptitude Test (SAT) and was at least five feet ten in height. The woman would be required to undergo thorough genetic screening and to offer several usable eggs for fertilization and transfer. Within a few days, more than two hundred women applied to be the donor.[10]

"I think we are moving to children as consumer products," said Lori Andrews, a Chicago law professor.[11] Nonsense, argued Norman Fost, head of the medical ethics program at the University of Wisconsin in Madison. He asserted that "whether children are valued and how they are treated has very little to do with how they are conceived."[12]

Given a Christian worldview commitment, based in a biblical understanding of the integrity of the marital bond, the integrity of the family, and the sanctity of human life—from the moment of chromosomal exchange to the moment of natural death—we cannot agree that all this has little to do with how children are conceived.

The excruciating pain of a married couple unable to conceive a child is understandable, but this does not mean that all technologies are therefore allowable or morally acceptable. Christian couples must not embrace the new reproductive technologies without clear biblical and theological reflection. At a bare minimum, Christian couples must commit to the implantation of all embryos, and the selective reduction of none. But this does not alter the fundamentally artificial character of the technology or the moral status of the embryos, and thus IVF presents grave moral issues to the Christian conscience. For these reasons, it should be avoided.

We must oppose the denial of human dignity to the unborn and often forgotten frozen embryos. We must oppose the use of these technologies by those who would subvert the family, the marital covenant, and the Creator's gift of sexual union and procreation. We must deny that what is technologically possible is therefore morally acceptable. We must affirm our creaturely limits and trust our gracious Creator as the Lord of Life who imposed those limits for our good. And we must learn to count the costs before those limitations are denied.

NOTES

1. For a detailed ethical discussion of this entire matter, see Beverly Wildung Harrison, *Our Right to Choose: Toward a New Ethic of Abortion* (Boston: Beacon Press, 1983), pp. 31ff.

2. Karl Rahner, "Experiment Man," *Theology Digest* 16 (February 1968): 60.

3. Karl Barth, *Church Dogmatics*, eds. G. W. Bromiley and T. F. Torrance (Edinburgh: T. and T. Clark, 1961).

4. These new technologies include gamete intrafallopian transfer (GIFT) and zygote intrafallopian transfer (ZIFT).

5. Oliver O'Donovan, *Begotten or Made?* (Oxford: Oxford University Press, 1984).

6. Paul Ramsey, *Fabricated Man: The Ethics of Genetic Control* (New Haven: Yale University Press, 1970), p. 149.

7. Of course human cloning would allow liberation even from the male as sperm donor. See R. Albert Mohler, Jr., "The Brave New World of Cloning," in *Human Cloning: Religious Responses*, ed. Ronald Cole-Turner (Louisville: Westminster/John Knox Press, 1997), pp. 91-105. The development of "egg fusion," which would combine genetic material from the eggs of two different women, would also achieve reproduction without male involvement, and would offer lesbian couples the opportunity to have a "shared" child.

8. Adam Cohen, "Test-Tube Tug-of-War," *Time*, 6 April 1998, p. 65.

9. Ezekiel J. Emanuel, M.D., Ph.D., "Eight Is Too Many," *The New Republic*, 25 January 1999, p. 11.

10. Gina Kolata, "$50,000 Offered to Tall, Smart Egg Donor," *New York Times*, 3 March 1999, sec. A, p. 10.

11. Ibid.

12. Ibid.

CHAPTER THREE

ARE "DESIGNER CHILDREN" AN ETHICAL CHOICE?

Overview

R esponding to the question "Are 'designer children' an ethical choice?" Ronald Cole-Turner and Marilyn E. Coors offer different but overlapping judgments. Neither proves to be absolutistic in opinion. Cole-Turner suggests that he is "saying yes while saying no"; and Coors, in essence, firmly says no while saying yes to certain dimensions of genetic engineering.

While "designer children" are not yet a reality, the scientific technology and possibilities are in the not-too-distant future. Highly sophisticated genetic treatments for the fetus *in utero* will soon be available. Germ-line modification appears on the horizon. The Human Genome Project increases the likelihood that in the future more diseases will be predictable and more pregnancies will be screened.

Cole-Turner worries about the inequitable costs, the dangers of babies becoming commodities, the loss of respect for human embryos, the potential complicity with biological determinism, and the threat of eugenics. Ethically, outweighing these concerns, however, is the possibility of preventing painful and fatal illnesses for infants. He asks, "Instead of treating a fetus that is already sick, why not start at conception and alter the genes in the embryo so that the genetic basis for the disease is eliminated entirely?" One can say yes to designer children within limits, rejecting worst-case scenarios. How it is used, not genetic technology itself, can be deemed morally wrong. Some uses can be justified; others not permitted. People of faith "can dare to offer even this new technology in the service of God."

Coors fears "producing made-to-order" children, and raises the issue of humans "playing God." Not discounting potential "advantageous outcomes in the production of designer babies" (for example, greater intelligence or eliminating violent tendencies), she does not believe the benefits outweigh the harms that genetic engineering could entail. She cites four reasons for opposition: (1) the reduction of human distinctiveness to genetic blueprints, (2) the loss of the sanctity of life by making it "an object of the marketplace," (3) the slide down a "slippery slope" toward Nazi-like eugenics, and (4) the lack of humility by which humans acknowledge they cannot fully calculate the consequences. Her "no" is qualified, in that she favors "the use of genetics for the purpose of generating health" and overcoming certain genetic illnesses.

ARE "DESIGNER CHILDREN" AN ETHICAL CHOICE?

A *Response by* Ronald Cole-Turner

"Designer babies" conjures up our worst fears about human genetics. The technology is not quite here yet, but it is foreseeable within a decade or so. Already, genetic testing is being combined with reproductive medicine to permit parents to select one embryo and reject another. In the first decade of the new century, we are likely to see genetic surgery done on fetuses *in utero*. And soon after that, human beings may be altered genetically at conception. If so, every cell in their bodies will be affected, and the alteration could pass to their children and grandchildren forever. Surely, it seems, designer babies are just around the corner. It's time to worry.

Reasons to Worry About Genetic Technologies

Five reasons people worry about these technologies can be cited:

First, technologies like these violate our sense of justice. How can we justify such expensive technologies to create babies for the privileged few when millions of children in the United States have inadequate health care, and hundreds of millions around the world live in poverty?

Second, reproductive technology reduces a baby to an engineering feat. The baby becomes a commodity, the person becomes a mere product, and pro*creation* becomes re*production*. A child created technologically becomes an expensive possession, something ordered and controlled, not an expression of love, full of risk and unpredictability.

Third, these technologies violate respect for the human embryo. Embryos should not be tested, manipulated, or discarded if they are genetically deficient. Whether we think of them as persons or only as "potential persons," they deserve profound respect. Selecting one and discarding another demeans them all.

Fourth, when we permit technologies like these, we show our complicity with biological determinism, which values genes and genetic connection above all else. People who buy into this believe that they must have a child who is genetically "their own," and so they are not open to adoption.

Fifth, allowing parents to select an embryo for genetic purposes is plain old eugenics, an attempt to improve human breeding. It doesn't matter that parents will do this freely, without government coercion. What matters is that they are trying to produce improved human beings. Surely this will lead to new forms of dominance and subservience.

These are serious worries, and they deserve careful exploration. And after reading them, you might be wondering: Why would anyone want to select the genes of their offspring? Why should anyone be allowed to design their children?

A Story from the Future

Let's start our discussion all over again, this time from a totally different starting point. Let's begin with a story from the future:

Ellen's first baby was born seriously ill and died within the first year of life. The doctors and the genetics counselor tell Ellen and her husband, Tom, that the problem is a rare genetic disease. In fact, the doctors say, most of the damage from the disease was caused before the baby was born, so the doctors assure Ellen and Tom that it was a "blessing" that their child did not live. The genetics counselor tells them that any future child of theirs might have the same disease.

After a few years, Ellen becomes pregnant, and she and Tom return to the genetics counselor to ask, "Is it possible for us to have a baby without risking this disease?"

"One way to do that," the genetics counselor tells them, "is to wait until the pregnancy is in about the twelfth week or so and then undergo a prenatal genetic test. If the test shows that there is a problem, you can end the pregnancy."

"And after I end the pregnancy, then what?" Ellen asks. "Try again and have another abortion? I would rather not have any children than to do it that way."

The genetics counselor describes an experimental procedure to try to correct the genetic problem early in the pregnancy. "If we wait until birth, it could be too late. Most of the damage, unfortunately, is done by then. The only chance is to try to correct the genes before the damage is done."

Tom and Ellen are interested, and so the next day they meet with the genetics counselor and with several physicians, including a pediatrician specializing in genetics, who does most of the talking.

"The first thing we will have to do is an amniocentesis, to make sure the problem is even there," she says. If there's no problem, then we'll all just sit back and wait for the happy news. If we are going to do any therapy, we want to make absolutely sure there's a problem."

"What happens next?" Ellen asks.

"The next step would be to try to inject millions of copies of corrected genes into the fetus," she says. "These genes will be carried inside special packages, called viral vectors.

We've learned how to take viruses, alter them so that they don't cause illness, and insert genes in them. These viral vectors help carry the genes into the cells, where they'll do some good. If all goes well, many of the corrected genes will get into the fetus, into just the right cells. And if that happens, it's quite possible that your baby will be born well. But to be very honest with you, we don't know for sure whether this will work. It's only been tried a few thousand times, here and in other medical centers. Some babies are born looking very healthy, but many others don't seem to be helped. And we don't know how well the healthy babies will be doing in five years or ten years. This is a new field for all of us."

"So in a way," Ellen says, "our baby would become a medical experiment. We really don't know whether this will do any good, right?"

"Of course it will do some good," Tom says. "Why else would they do it?"

"Actually, Ellen's closer to being right," the doctor says. "We have some good reasons to be hopeful, but we can't say for sure that this will do any good for your baby."

"But it will help you learn? You'll learn something from treating our baby that will help others?" Ellen asks.

"Yes," the doctor says. "We certainly hope so. That's why we do this work. Now there are a couple of other things you should know. First, Ellen, this won't be easy to go through. In order to treat the fetus, we have to insert medical instruments into your uterus. We'll go over all these steps very carefully and make sure you understand everything and are comfortable with the risks you'll be exposed to. And finally, you need to know that if we succeed in treating your baby, and if your baby grows up and has children of his or her own, there's a possibility that what we do will affect them. Some of the corrected genes might find their way into the developing egg or sperm precursor cells inside the fetus and be passed on to your grandchildren."

"I'm not sure I'm following," Tom says. "Will that make

our grandchildren sick, or will it keep them from getting sick?"

"Well, again, we can't say for sure," says the doctor, "because no baby ever treated this way has had time to live long enough to have children. We're not sure it will make any difference at all, but we can't rule that out. A corrected gene may find its way into an egg or a sperm cell. And if that happens, it could mean that your grandchild would not have the disease and would not pass it on."

"Is that a problem?" asks Tom. "I mean, wouldn't that be a good thing?"

"In some ways, yes," says the doctor. "But I have to tell you that many people find it pretty sobering to think that our medical intervention, our genetic modification, will have consequences for generation after generation, possibly forever. Quite frankly, that scares a lot of people. After all, we might be affecting your child's germ line. We wouldn't be trying to do that, but we have to recognize that we could be engaged here in unintended germ-line modification."

"By 'germ-line modification,' you mean it could affect our grandchildren and their grandchildren, maybe forever?" Ellen asks.

"That's right," the doctor says.

Prevention of Fatal Illness

This story is not yet true. But when we think about the story and about people like Ellen and Tom, the worries we listed before do not seem to get at the heart of the story. What touches us here is not eugenics or technology gone mad, but Ellen and Tom's deep desire to have a baby free of the terrible disease that killed their first baby. They want to use a new technology to achieve that desire. *They want to prevent a fatal illness, not design their baby. They watched their first baby die, and they do not want to go through that again.* How are we to respond to their pain? But we must be careful here: If we say yes to Ellen and Tom and let them use technology to prevent a fatal disease, must we then say yes to someone else who wants to use it for less worthy purposes? Are we about to be seduced into technological permissiveness by our own compassion? Must we, in order to say no to bad uses, say no to every use, and thereby say no to the technology itself? Or can we learn to say yes and no to this technology, yes to its good uses and no to its bad uses? I believe we can.

Dangers of Germ-Line Modifications

We have very little time to decide. The opening decade of the new century will be a critical moment in human history. In that decade we may begin to use genetic technology to alter ourselves profoundly. The technique Ellen and Tom considered has already been proposed and publicly debated by government oversight agencies.[1]

Before too long, many couples may find themselves in the position of Ellen and Tom. They will be offered highly sophisticated genetic treatments for the fetus *in utero*. They may be warned that these techniques might result in germ-line modification, even if that is not directly intended.

Depending on how patients and families respond and how the general public reacts, it is possible, perhaps even likely, that in another five years or so we will see a proposal for intended germ-line modification. Instead of treating a fetus that is already sick, why not start at conception and alter the genes in the embryo so that the genetic basis for the disease is eliminated entirely? Techniques for doing this have been used in animals and have already been proposed for use in human beings.

We need to be careful here about how the technology will evolve. It's not very likely that we'll wake up some morning and hear that a designer baby has been born. The technology is not likely to take such flying leaps. It will inch forward, bit by bit, from one microgoal to the next, with decisions too small to be noticed by most of us.

And we can be sure that the technology will also evolve according to certain rules of public approval. Right now the public would not tolerate designer babies, at least not in the sense of improving human genes at conception in order to enhance physical and mental traits. The recent science-fiction movie *Gattaca* warned of some of the dangers that could lie ahead. In the film, people who were conceived the old-fashioned way are discriminated against by those who were genetically enhanced. Currently, it is publicly acceptable to treat illness through genetic enhancement, so we can be sure that the technology will develop first for that purpose. However, if enhancement goes farther, the public may have misgivings. The problem, of course, is that once the technology is developed, it can be used for other purposes. The technique used to prevent disease can also be used to make a "better" human being.

How far could it go? Consider the prediction of Lee Silver, a prominent scientist working in this field. Referring to a time about two centuries from now, he writes: "It was a critical turning point in the evolution of life in the universe. . . . Throughout it all, there were those who said we couldn't go any farther, that there were limits to mental capacity and technological advances. But those prophesied limits were swept aside, one after another, as intelligence, knowledge, and technological power continued to rise." Silver is suggesting that our offspring, if enhanced, will be able to enhance their offspring even further. Then he points to a time more than a millennium away: "A special point has now been reached in the distant future. And in this era, there exists a special group of mental beings. Although these beings can trace their ancestry back directly to *homo sapiens,* they are as different from humans as humans are from the primitive worms with tiny brains that first crawled along the earth's surface."[2]

Judge Not Technology, But Its Use

Nevertheless, in spite of such possibilities, we must insist that it is not the technology but its use that we must judge morally. This is generally true of technology. A telephone can be used to plan a crime or to share a moment of prayer. The Internet can convey pornography or medical advice. It is not the telephone or the Internet or genetic engineering that is good or bad, but the uses to which we put these things. This is generally true of technology, I suggested, because I do not want to fall here for the guns-don't-kill-people argument. Some technologies are designed for bad uses. Switchblades, biological weapons, handguns, crack cocaine, and nuclear weapons have all been put into that category. The question here is whether human genetic modification belongs in that category, too. Is it a bad technology regardless of its use, or is it, like most technologies, usable for bad or good purposes?

I believe this technology may have good uses. It may be possible to use it to prevent diseases that currently cause great pain and suffering and early death. We do not have to defend Silver's visions in order to permit people like Ellen and Tom to use these techniques to have a baby who will not die in the first year of life. We can permit some uses without permitting them all.

The most important questions to ask about this technology, or about any technology, are these: What is God making possible through the development of this technology? What new forms of action are becoming possible? How might God act in us and through us, using this technology? Is our use of the technology consistent with God's claim upon us?

Saying Yes While Saying No

We can decide, use by use, case by case, what is proper and what is not. Instead of saying "Absolutely not," we can take a yes-and-no approach. "Absolutely not" is both incorrect and ineffective. It is incorrect in that it rejects the possibility that God may find good uses in all creation, in all human action, and in all our work. It is a repudiation of the possibility of new forms of God's presence and mercy. It is a rejection of the idea that if we human beings are creative, God is even more creative and can create through us. "Absolutely not" is also ineffective. Those who adopt it will find it inconsequential in preventing the very misuses they worry so much about. It will not prevent the development and widespread legal use of technology. All it will do is to put the technology under a cloud of suspicion. Under that cloud, all uses will be bad, so we need not distinguish good purposes from bad. To take this view is to abdicate the ethics of the details. Saying "Absolutely not" will define these technologies as inherently godless. The result will be faith versus technology, as if one must choose one or the other, as if we cannot be people of faith who make responsible and faithful choices about how to use technology and about how to welcome God's action in our lives through technology.

We need to learn to live as people of faith amidst the technological revolutions of our time, to use these technologies to the extent that they are consistent with our life of faith, and to reject them when they are not. We need to do this in conversation with one another in our communities of faith. And we need to decide these matters in public and to let others know what we think.

We also need to imagine misuses and talk about why the technologies would be bad. We need to keep all our worries about these technologies clearly in mind, especially when we find ourselves moved by sympathy to say yes to people like Ellen and Tom. But sometimes yes is the right answer, and so we need to use technology responsibly—to say yes and no to it in such a way that encourages other people, those of other faiths or of no religious conviction, to make responsible choices, too.

Genetic Technology in the Service of God

Does God care whether we use such technologies as *in utero* gene therapy and human germ-line modification? Very much indeed! Some years ago I wrote a hymn that is used in many churches when a child is baptized. This is the third stanza:

> Child of joy, our dearest treasure,
> God's you are, from God you came.
> Back to God we humbly give you;
> Live as one who bears Christ's name.[3]

In far more majestic words, the psalmist, addressing God, affirms, "You . . . formed my inward parts; you knit me together in my mother's womb" (Psalm 139:13).

And precisely because that is true, we can dare to offer even this new technology in the service of God.

NOTES

1. Gene Therapy Policy Conference; French Anderson preliminary proposal.

2. Lee Silver, *Remaking Eden: How Genetic Engineering and Cloning Will Transform the American Family* (New York: Avon Books, 1998), pp. 292-93.

3. Ronald Cole-Turner, "Child of Blessing, Child of Promise," 1981.

ARE "DESIGNER CHILDREN" AN ETHICAL CHOICE?

A Response by Marilyn E. Coors

Babies come in many colorful sizes, shapes, and styles. Should parents be able to designate those attributes that they desire for their child? Until recently this question was so far-fetched it was not worth asking. The only way a person could choose the characteristics of her or his children was to choose a mate with admirable characteristics and hope the offspring turned out to be as smart or as good-looking as the person or the person's spouse. This method, called selective breeding, only occasionally resulted in producing a child who looked or behaved just as the parents intended. However, recent advances in genetic science suggest that in the near future it may be possible to create a designer baby more efficiently by means of genetic engineering.

Producing Made-to-Order Children

Genetic engineering originally meant the introduction of healthy genes into the cells of a particular organ, with the intent of correcting illness. With recent scientific advances, the scope of genetic engineering has expanded to include the possibility of producing a made-to-order child. This practice entails the alteration of the genes in a fertilized egg so that during development all of the child's cells will receive a gene(s) that the parents choose to bequeath. Genetic options could include the alteration of physical attributes, mentioned above, or the elimination of an inherited disorder, such as cystic fibrosis. The opportunity to alter genes provides humans the means to be involved in the creation and manipulation of life with a degree of efficiency and specificity that was not possible in less technological means of human reproduction.

Many believe that we are poised on the brink of seizing control of our own evolution, or "playing God." As humans begin to alter their genes in precise and permanent ways, science is accused of supplanting the role of the divine, of crossing the line between the created and the creator. Changes introduced in the genes of a fertilized egg not only will potentially affect the egg and sperm cells of the ensuing child, but will be inherited by his or her children, grandchildren, and distant offspring, thus touching the very core of human identity.

Crossing Ethical and Theological Boundaries

For most scientists, ethicists, and theologians the genetic engineering of human eggs and sperm cross a boundary that is fraught with ethical barriers. Traditional Jewish and Christian religious beliefs embrace a God who is both omniscient (knowing everything) and omnipotent (having unlimited power and authority), and who has created the world with a preordained purpose. Genetic engineers are charged with playing God when they attempt to assume powers for which they possess no authority, or at least insufficient wisdom. As this occurs, some believe that ethics and human life in general will embark on uncharted and potentially perilous territory.

Others take issue with the disparaging implications of the idea of playing God based on the idea's abstract nature and alleged intent to shock. Their rebuttal: Doctors play God every time they treat an illness. All of medicine involves subjecting the human body to some type of alteration.

In many ways this assertion is correct. However, the ability to change the tools of heredity links human power with irrevocability. The hand of humankind now has the potential to control human life in an unprecedented fashion.

Many ethical issues can be cited to document the dangers entailed in the production of children with made-to-order genes. An important consideration central to the argument opposing the production of designer babies is the principle of justice. Parents desiring to design their offspring according to their personal preference will need to possess considerable wealth in order to afford such services. This reality generates the ethical anxiety that only rich families will be able to improve their genetic traits. A procedure that neglects the poor or defenseless, and/or widens the gap between the haves and have-nots is problematic, especially in a culture obsessed with the importance of the competitive edge. Genetic improvements in appearance, strength, and/or stamina could give some children advantages over those who are unimproved, further intensifying already existing inequalities.

Objecting to Human Manufacturing of Babies

This is not to negate the possibility of advantageous outcomes in the production of designer babies. Individuals could potentially be produced with the intelligence to solve the problems of disease, pollution, and many other societal concerns. Possibly, genes that control behavior could be altered to eliminate violent or aggressive tendencies, and/or these genes could potentially be turned "on" and "off" at will. If this becomes reality, the outrages of crime and the indignities of incarceration could potentially be eliminated. However, it is my contention that although the potential for good is possible, benefit alone cannot justify the production of designer children, nor overcome the harms that human genetic engineering could entail. Four concerns compose the basis of the argument opposing the production of designer babies. By citing genetic blueprints, sanctity of life, the slippery slope, and the virtue of humility, I will demonstrate the religious and philosophic grounds for objecting to the manufacture of babies according to human design.

Genetic blueprints. First, in terms of genetic blueprints, human life can be described exclusively in terms of genes and genetic information. Genes direct the cellular production of the chemicals necessary for life. Human beings can be viewed as nothing more than information systems, comparable to a computer operating on a program prescribed by its heredity. Following this reasoning, nature can be likened to a system of storage and transmission of information. As such, a simple change in the information base could produce a predictable change in outcomes.

The imagery of genetic blueprints and cellular machinery illustrates a new way of thinking that could reduce the distinctiveness of the individual to his/her genetic components. Once the genetic code is deciphered, it would be possible to explain all human characteristics in terms of a genetic language; this includes both health and behavior. This outlook could result in the overstatement of the role that heredity plays in human existence, and the dismissal of the possibility of a spiritual component to human life. A genetic blueprint disregards the mysterious heights and the mystic depths that compose the human soul. Persons of no particular religious tradition place a high value on human life, but the religious assessment of life adds the value of the spiritual dimension of human beings. Thus, there is wariness toward a genetic program that could potentially reduce human existence to a DNA code.

Sanctity of life. Second, the religious grounding of the doctrine of the sanctity of life rests in the belief that human beings were created in the image of God, and as such possess incomparable dignity (Genesis 1:27). This conviction manifests the source of worth conferred upon all humankind. As the production of human children moves toward the realm of human invention, the concern is that life will be viewed as an object of the marketplace rather than as a gift from God.

The production of a genetically modified child aims at satisfying real or perceived human needs through systematic genetic choices. Parents select the attributes of their child just as a calculating consumer chooses the specifications desired in an automobile or a computer. The human child can be compared to a product that is ordered, paid for, and delivered as specified. Judaism and Christianity historically have condemned the practice of selling human organs or babies, or in any way reducing life to a monetary value. Many believe that the breech of this taboo in the arena of human genetics could have an impact on other values not recognized by the market. These are values that revere life as more than genes, and well-being as more than prosperity.

Philosophers, who espouse the belief that humans are to be treated as ends in themselves, subsequently hold that objectifying or commodifying the human child is immoral or unethical. Philosopher Immanuel Kant formulated the most influential secular principle establishing human dignity.[1] Kant asserted the realization that all rational beings are to be treated as ends in themselves, and not merely as means. This imperative would prohibit the reduction of children to a market commodity or the mere object of their parents' whims or wishes.

Slippery slope. Third, ethicists use "slippery slope" to describe the inevitable slide from practices that are ethically questionable to those that are clearly unethical. The implication is that once a boundary has been crossed, it becomes impossible to reinstitute means to prevent unacceptable practices. The imagery of the slippery slope represents the conviction that the approval of ethically questionable practices, such as the improvement of intelligence, will lead to other utilizations that are unethical, such as the practice of eugenics.

Eugenics, the planned improvement of the human race through the breeding of better human beings, has received considerable attention in the popular media with reference to genetic engineering. These allegations have produced both unjustified fear and rational apprehension. The term *eugenics* immediately brings to mind the discriminatory and brutal programs carried out in Nazi Germany during World War II. What began as an effort to eliminate genetic disorders through involuntary sterilization culminated in an evil attempt to exterminate a nationality that was deemed "genetically unfit."

It is feared that the production of designer babies, which focuses on the goal of perfection, will lead to the elimination of human hereditary differences that are perceived to be undesirable. This could include differences in sexual orientation, racial characteristics, or inherited disabilities. Society could become separated into those individuals who are genetically superior and those who are genetically unfit. Those deemed acceptable would be candidates for the best jobs, and insurance; the less desirable could be cast aside because of disabilities that impose financial or social costs on society. Thus, the use of the new genetics could entail harm as well as good. History reveals that knowledge about heredity is susceptible to exploitation by those with self-serving or unscrupulous motives.

Leroy Walters, professor of Christian ethics at Georgetown University, illustrates this concern, speculating that genetic engineering is not likely to be used to create a super-race of geniuses. Instead, he fears that it could be used for malicious purposes. He commented that it is usually easier to make things inferior than to make improvements.[2] Walters is concerned that, in the hands of an immoral government, genetic engineering could be used to create a class of slaves with lessened mental and physical abilities to perform the undesirable or dangerous tasks in society.

This anxiety is based on the perceived social power of genetic information to generate a new lower class through the creation of social categories based on the presence or absence of certain genes. For example, persons could be discriminated against because they have nontreatable genetic illnesses, or because they carry an undesirable gene and intend to have children. Given the heinous history of eugenics in the twentieth century, the apprehensions evoked by the enhancement or the degradation of humans are difficult to dismiss. The fear that scientists will have the ability to completely remake human beings is probably unjustified, based on the enormous complexity of human genes. However, it is naive to suppose that once knowledge is gained, it will not be used in some fashion.

Humility. Fourth, the virtue of humility, often overlooked and particularly unpopular in the postmodern age, needs a revitalization in light of the tremendous power that genetic engineering has the potential to manifest. Hans Jonas, philosopher from Hitler's Germany, describes a "new kind of humility" that correlates with the measure of human power present in the ability to change our genes and possibly our destiny.[3] The new humility differs from former interpretations of humility in that it focuses not on the insignificance of human ability, but on the magnitude of our capacity to achieve. The new humility emphasizes the ways in which our power to act exceeds the ability to understand and evaluate the consequences of actions. The nearly unlimited potential to change the inherited qualities of humanity is coupled with a limited ability to grasp what those changes will ultimately entail. The virtue of humility is key if we are to understand the imbalance between that which can be accomplished and that which should be.

Human DNA is incredibly complex. It is possible that alterations in DNA could interrupt a good gene or introduce some unknown gene into the stream of human life. It is also possible that some valuable immune-enhancing gene could be unintentionally eradicated, or some unplanned side effects could occur. For example, it is presently known that the gene that causes sickle cell anemia also carries immunity against malaria. The elimination of this gene for the purpose of preventing disease eradicates its beneficial aspects as well. If the sickle cell gene carries both harm and good, what unexpected side effects lurk in changes to other genes?

One has to question whether the control of heredity should ever be placed in human hands. Catholic moral thought objects to human control of heredity based on the argument that inherited genetic changes pose a threat to human nature. The fear is that the combined effect of genetic changes over many generations could result in human beings that are unlike us. This claim is rooted in the belief that there is a human essence that can be recognized and forms the basis for natural law. As such, human nature is illustrative of what God meant to be good for humans, and attempts to tamper with nature are in conflict with the divine purpose of creation.

Reflecting About God's Perspective

Reflecting about God's perspective on how we make babies with technology is the primary purpose of this chapter, focusing specifically on the ethical assessment of the creation of designer babies. In summation, the production of designer babies leads humans down a path that could seriously compromise human dignity through the diminishing of life to a market commodity based only upon genes. We have also seen that genetic engineering entails the tremendous temptation to usurp the role of the Creator by taking control of the destiny of future persons without the wisdom to do so. Perhaps the most tangible objection is the probability that the beneficial uses of genetic improvement will drift into uses that are harmful and clearly unethical. The very presence of these serious concerns underscores the evidence that the production of designer babies is most likely beyond the boundary of that which God intended as the human domain.

This is not to say that we should ever abandon the attempt to improve our children. Improving our world and our offspring is central to human progress. The point is that the most preferable path to this goal may not lie solely in our DNA. Faith in the possibility of genetic programming of children could encourage parents to overvalue currently fashionable traits and devalue others. Suffice it to say that our current ideals of perfection are not always so admirable. Our culture pursues notions of perfection defined by fashion magazines, TV soap operas, and sports heroes. It is readily apparent that these idols may not translate well into the distant future.

Does this mean that God opposes all attempts at genetic engineering in humans? I would answer this question with a "yes," with the exception of genetic illnesses such as cystic fibrosis, Tay-Sachs, or Huntington's disease. God has granted humans dominion over creation and promised us a better world in which pain and suffering is diminished (Genesis 1:28; Matthew 4:23). The accounts of Jesus healing the sick are plentiful in Scripture, and he commands his followers to do the same (Matthew 10:1). The search for a life free from devastating genetic illness is central to this vision of God's kingdom on earth. For this reason, the use of genetics for the purpose of generating health should be endorsed.

In contrast, other purposes for genetically engineering a human should be rejected as unethical. The desire for a baby designed according to someone's fleeting idea of human perfection has the potential to devalue human dignity. The ominous threat is that, in pursuit of a better world, those in control will not implement genetic engineering in conjunction with God's creative purpose of healing and blessing. It will be a grave injustice if the ability to change our genes, which holds the potential to ameliorate genetic illness, results in new forms of intolerance and injustice.

NOTES

1. See Immanuel Kant, *Groundwork of the Metaphysics of Morals*, trans. H. J. Paton (New York: Harper & Bros., 1956), esp. p. 95.
2. See Craig Donnegan, "Gene Therapy's Future," *The Congressional Quarterly Researcher* 5 (8 December 1995): 1006.
3. See Hans Jonas, *Philosophical Essays* (Englewood Cliffs, N.J.: Prentice Hall, 1974), esp. p. 78.

QUESTIONS

1. How do you interpret the biblical struggles with infertility, surrogacy, and pregnancy terminations?
2. Do you know anyone who has utilized some type of reproductive technology (for example, in vitro fertilization, egg or sperm donation, and so forth)? What were their experiences? What are your feelings about their experiences?
3. If the technology were available, would a couple, knowing that a serious genetic disease such as Tay-Sachs exists in the family, be morally justified in requesting genetic alteration of a fetus at risk of inheriting the disease?
4. Would it be morally appropriate to eliminate diseases in the unborn, but ethically inappropriate to designate the height, gender, sexual orientation, and other characteristics of a child? Why? Why not?
5. It is unlikely that assisted reproduction can be prohibited, even if such prohibition seemed morally justifiable. How should faith communities be involved in helping (caring for) those involved—the donors, the rearing parents, and the children?

PART TWO

ABORTION:
AN AGONIZING DEBATE

CHAPTER FOUR

WHEN DOES LIFE BEGIN?

Ruth L. Fuller, M.D.

R esolved: Abortion is murder. Affirmative? Negative? In this section, the thinking of diverse groups of concerned individuals is being presented on the subject of abortion (when an expected new life ends), and the more difficult subject of when new life begins. I suggest that we turn our attention to what may seem to be some obvious questions.

Some Obvious Questions

First, what is abortion? Even a brief medical definition of abortion—"[t]he termination of pregnancy before the stage of viability" or survival outside of the uterus—is followed by a list of different kinds of abortion: for example, habitual (recurrent), missed, threatened, and selective removal of one or more embryos in a multiple pregnancy.

The repeated references to the viability of the fetus bring us to the second question: When is the embryo or fetus sufficiently developed to survive outside of the uterus and thus become a baby, a person? Twenty years ago, the answer to the question was spelled out quite clearly: "Between the twentieth and twenty-eighth week of [pregnancy]" and, among other factors, "a fetus . . . weighing less than 500 grams [1.1 pounds]."[1]

Over the last two decades, we have witnessed an explosion in the technology for caring for tiny infants (no longer called embryos) of a birth weight and duration of pregnancy that had been seen as incompatible with life. The length of pregnancy needed to presume survival of the premature baby is now twenty-seven weeks, and non-survivability of an aborted fetus to be less than twenty weeks. The "gray area," if you will, is between twenty and twenty-seven weeks, because sometimes survival is possible.[2]

This gray area presents difficult ethical questions. Should every effort be made to save all babies born during this problematic period? Some persons believe the answer is, yes, save the baby at all cost. At the other extreme are those who feel that efforts to save these babies are futile and should be minimized. These persons cite the enormous financial cost of neonatal care as well as the high risk of severe physical and/or mental impairments common in infants born during this "gray area."

A third approach is to assess each of these situations on merit. Both physical and psychosocial assessment are highly desirable. Psychiatrists or chaplains can help families by first understanding their wishes and then assisting the family in understanding the medical and psychosocial realities of their situation.

Parents who have rejoiced in the pregnancy from the earliest moments of awareness will wish to have all that medicine can offer to help save their baby or babies. If the medical prognosis for the infant is good, the family will applaud the medical miracle that saved their baby. If the infant is in poor condition and deteriorating, the psychiatrist or chaplain may need to help the family begin to come to closure on the life of the baby they had expected to nurture to adulthood.

For the single, pregnant adolescent or young woman, or the single or married mother of several children, or the menopausal woman who does not see childbearing as a wonderful "miracle," the wish not to be pregnant is intense. In these situations, the potential mother may not go to the hospital "too soon" during a miscarriage or potential abortion. Numerous such potential mothers have said to me that they quietly listened to the emergency room staff's criticism of them summed up as, "You should have come sooner. We might have saved the baby." Privately, they tolerated such naïveté as one of the difficulties that some persons of privilege have when they cannot put themselves in someone else's shoes. After getting to the hospital "too late to save the baby," one young woman put it very clearly: "They [the emergency room staff] did not understand that the last thing that I wanted to hear was 'You got here just in time.' "

Late-Term Abortion

Aborting a viable fetus presents yet another ethical controversy. The development of a medical procedure called an "intact dilatation and evacuation" has raised a storm of controversy. You will read about this procedure in more detail in the following chapter. Briefly, the intact dilatation and evacuation (also referred to as "partial-birth abortion") comes under fierce scrutiny because it is performed during the time of the "gray area" and beyond (during the fourth to ninth month of pregnancy). For some of us, this possible medical procedure is never acceptable. However, always and never are two absolutes and difficult to maintain. We look for a consensus.

Making Consensus Definitions

Such a search brings us to our third question: What factors influence the making of consensus definitions and rules of behavior? Guidelines for the legality and acceptability of inducing or performing an abortion have varied with societies around the world and at various points in history. Today, think of the citizens in Greece in the fourth and fifth century B.C. finding it necessary to have included in the Hippocratic oath for physicians that "I will give no deadly medicine to anyone if asked, nor suggest any such counsel; and in like manner I will not give a woman a pessary to produce abortion."[3]

Jumping forward to the recent history of the United States, we can note that abortion was legal in this country until 1828 when antiabortion laws were passed by some states. The original intent of these laws was to protect women from dangerous surgery and infection, since antiseptic surgery would arrive in the future. At the same time, midwives in larger numbers (women) were more available to women than doctors (generally men and in smaller numbers). Economics, as well as safety, influenced doctors' attitude toward abortion. Doctors needed to make a living in the practice of medicine, and midwives "diverted" too many patients into their own practices.

As could have been predicted by students of history, once abortion became illegal, except under highly restricted circumstances, a large, underground practice of abortion developed. In 1970, the *Nixon Report* on organized crime listed illegal abortions as the third largest moneymaker for organized crime.[4] There is no comment about the neighborhood abortionist who was not a part of organized crime, or of the regional expert abortionist who ran the risk of breaking the law by providing "safe" abortions as a protest against the dangerously amateur, self-proclaimed abortionist.

Out of the Civil Rights and Human Rights movements in this country, the Women's Movement of the 1970s had large numbers of women successfully demanding that the issue of abortion be really an issue of constitutional rights. When *Roe v. Wade* was decided in January 1973, the judicial vote was 7 to 2, reflecting a strong consensus among the members of the Supreme Court at that time.[5] The challengers to this decision feel as passionately about what the law should be, as do the supporters.

The Experiences of Patients

Adolescents and women tell many stories about experiences with abortion, legal and illegal. One woman, Alice, age thirty-six, told of her pain in finding out that her infected, illegal abortion at age seventeen had most likely given rise to sterility problems that were not being overcome. She felt profound guilt about "the baby [she] had murdered" and inconsolable grief for the babies that she would never have.

Another story about obtaining a legal abortion is that of fourteen-year-old Sarah. When I, as a psychiatrist, first saw Sarah, Mrs. M., her mother, was applying for her daughter to have an abortion in a hospital in about the nineteenth week of pregnancy (because the pregnancy had only recently been diagnosed). Furthermore, when Sarah was convinced that she really was pregnant, she became very depressed. When Sarah was raped, she had said nothing about it, because she felt responsible for the attack. She had unlocked the door when she was at home alone, because a uniformed man tricked her into thinking that he was the authorized plumber called to fix a problem. Mrs. M. tried to reassure Sarah that she was not responsible for either the attack or the pregnancy.

Mrs. M. summarized her pain for her daughter and her own feeling of helplessness in trying to follow the prescribed steps for a "legal" abortion. She cried as she passionately presented her understanding of the stakes:

> "We are poor and we are black. Everyone else here except you is white. They look at Sarah and say, 'Raped indeed.' Why is it so hard to believe that there are fourteen-year-old black virgins who think

enough of themselves to leave sex for the future when they are ready to handle it? That was my Sarah. Some animal came and took that away from my child. This baby would not be her baby, conceived in love. I could not look at that baby and not hate it. It may be unchristian, but I cannot love and forgive that much. When self-righteous white people say that Sarah should have the baby and place it for adoption, I want to scream, 'Is that what you would do to your daughter?' I wouldn't even try to point out that there would be one more black baby that probably no one adopts.

"Now Sarah has to be evaluated again by psychiatrists to see if she is really depressed or not, dangerous to herself or not. The longer these evaluations take, the longer she is pregnant, until, God forbid, she is then told that she waited too long for an abortion. If I had the money to take her to another country in which abortion is legal, we would have been there and back by now. I can't take her to the local, illegal abortionist. I don't want to have my child suffer in a back alley, or lose her altogether."

Sarah did have an abortion. Her immediate response was one of profound relief that she was believed and that she was no longer pregnant.

Mrs. M. presented biological, psychological, and social ideas about procreation, including when life begins. At fourteen years of age, Sarah was biologically able to become pregnant. Psychologically, she had an investment in not becoming "another" pregnant teenager. Sarah had not been sexually active, because her community's expectation is that if she were to become a teen mother, then the family would take care of her child. She felt that another person to care for would be too great a burden for her already overworked mother. For Mrs. M. and

Sarah, a new life begins when there is a baby, not a pregnancy with a fetus. The preparation for a new life, a baby, is expected to be through love. Physical assault is not preparation for a baby. Socially, relatives, friends, and their church family supported the M. family's pursuit of an abortion for Sarah.

Understanding Divergent Ideas and Multiple Births

A fourth question is, How do we approach understanding divergent ideas? In taking the position of listening to persons who may disagree with us, the listeners have the opportunity to reconsider what they had thought to be "obvious," "self-evident," or "true." We come to these questions with different experiences borne out of different realities, not one shared reality. For example, a colleague from a village in rural east Africa reminded the Western physicians that concepts and expectations are different in a setting in which survival to the first or even the fifth birthday is not an expected given. Similarly, expectations concerning any medical care are extremely modest.

Recently, communications about multiple births have increased. Opinions seen in articles and interviews cover a wide range of feelings; for example, any child is a gift from God;[6] all babies, no matter how many, are gifts;[7] "eight is more than enough";[8] "God did not do it, science did."[9] From some quarters of society, we hear criticism of couples who want to abort one or more fertilized eggs or embryos when there are a high number of embryos. The couple's thinking includes a respect for the actual limitations in the design of the female reproductive system and body. The other consideration is for their future child or children. They wish to increase the likelihood of having at least one or two robust babies at birth rather than many tiny babies that do not survive or who have lifetime special needs. As far as the female body is concerned, there are physical limitations to how much the uterus can stretch, the abdominal cavity can hold, the physiology of the mother can change in order to provide nutrients, and the workload the mother's organs can tolerate.

When Does a Fetus Become a Baby?

And so, we come to our last question: When does life as a separate, conscious person begin, or when does a fetus become a baby? The short answer to this question is that I do not know. At the same time, some of us consider the answer to be obvious through the teachings of a particular society or faith system; for example, at the instant of conception, with the first intrauterine movements, or with the first breath or cry.[10]

Longer discussions of theological views are found within this entire book. One consideration that comes from the sciences may be quite helpful to us. In the book *The Facts of Life,* the definition of the words *human being* and *humanness* point to a possible "when and why" a fetus (a potential life) becomes a new person (a new, separate, conscious individual). It is noted that the cerebral cortex begins to function during the twenty-fourth and thirty-second weeks of pregnancy.[11] Rephrased, it is in the transition from nonviable, through the questionably viable, to the clearly viable period of pregnancy that the higher brain functions begin. The significance of this biological development is that consciousness or a state of awareness should be biologically impossible without the development of this part of the brain.[12] At this point in our history, we are really relative neophytes at gathering observed information about mental functioning in the infant.

Western technology has rapidly changed and challenged previous understandings of when viable life begins and what abortion means. Fixation on the fetus should not obscure our focus on the ethics of applied technology. These highly sophisticated techniques may or may not enhance the quality of life. Could some of our intellectual and financial resources be better spent caring for existing children suffering from malnutrition and abuse? Are not questions about the quality of young lives as important to ask in tandem with queries about the beginning of life?

NOTES

1. *Taber's Cyclopedic Medical Dictionary*, ed. C. L. Thomas (Philadelphia: Davis Company, 1977), s.v. "abortion."
2. D. Finkel, "What Do You Think the Chances Are?" *Washington Post Magazine*, 27 October 1991, pp. 11-17, 24-28.
3. *Taber's*, s.v. "Hippocratic oath."
4. S. Weddington, *A Question of Choice* (New York: Penguin Books, 1993), p. 40.
5. Ibid., p. 146.
6. J. Bottum, "Facing Up to Infanticide," *First Things*, vol. 60 (1996): 41-44.
7. T. Langford, "Mom Slept Upside Down to Prolong Pregnancy," *Denver Post*, 22 December 1998, sec. A, p. 6.
8. K. Parker, "Eight Is More Than Enough," *Denver Post*, 27 December 1998, sec. G, p. 3.
9. Ibid.
10. S. Poliwoda, *Bioethical Problems in the Definition of the Beginning of Life in Judaism* (Germany: Diskussionsforum Medizinische Ethik, 1993), pp. xiii-xiv.
11. H. J. Morowitz and J. S. Trefil, *The Facts of Life* (Oxford: Oxford University Press, 1992).
12. *Taber's*, s.v. "consciousness."

CHAPTER FIVE

IS ABORTION EVER A LEGITIMATE MORAL CHOICE?

Overview

The agonizing debate over abortion clearly divides religious persons of faith. The different ways persons answer the question when life begins proves to be decisive in the discussion. Psychiatrist Ruth L. Fuller, M.D., clearly states that no scientific consensus exists as to when life as a separate, conscious person begins or when a fetus becomes a baby. The United States Supreme Court, in *Roe v. Wade,* has reached a compromise judgment as to when abortions are constitutional and legal, but individuals still must make up their own minds based on ethical and theological judgments.

United Methodist Bishop Judith Craig and Hastings Center Catholic ethicist Sidney Callahan provide opposing answers to the question of whether abortion is ever a legitimate moral choice. Although their responses are distinctly different, they both make exceptions in their ethical stances. Craig rejects casual decision making for convenience' sake, and Callahan permits abortion to save a woman's life or health in emergency situations.

Craig pushes readers to face the real-life dramas of unwanted and difficult pregnancies. Far from idealizing abortion, she speaks of the "holy potential" and "God-likeness of human life" that is embodied in a fetus. However, with reluctance she accepts tragic human realities in a less-than-perfect world. Living with ethical ambiguities, not absolutes, she chooses to stand with the agonizing woman who ultimately must make a decision. She doubts that one can ever say "never." Extreme circumstances legitimate making the "terrible choice for abortion." Thus she favors legal, safe, and compassionate avenues for abortion.

Callahan argues that abortion on request is never a legitimate choice, because it "extinguishes human life and violates the moral demand for equal and just treatment for all members of humanity." Aborting tiny embryos equates to killing babies. Late abortions amount to infanticide. Children are not "products of their parents' will," but gifts with "their own inalienable rights to life." Because women have a right to life too, Callahan grants an exception with "her life or health in emergencies," but she rejects abortion in cases of rape and incest, apparently favoring, if necessary, giving the child up for adoption.

IS ABORTION EVER A LEGITIMATE MORAL CHOICE?

A Response by Judith Craig

Television commercials promoting home pregnancy confirmation kits are full of sentimental and idealized images, designed to stir up in us a sense of, "Oh, isn't that wonderful!" And it is wonderful—wonderful to see the look come over the always beautiful young woman's face, and the gleam of awe and pride wash into the eyes of the inevitably handsome father-to-be. There they are, the perfect couple, wanting a child, ready to receive a child, and both brimming with the appropriate wonder and delight that accompanies that moment of discovery that "We are pregnant!"

When God created male and female and set forth a process for reproduction of humankind, I wonder if God also envisioned those moments of first knowing. Did God foresee the delight, the gratitude of a wish fulfilled, the huge expansion of imagination that comes when a couple learns "We are pregnant!" I like to think so. I like to think that is what God intended with the good gift of reproductive possibility. Such a vision of God's dream for humankind corresponds to the God of grace and joy and delight in life whom I know from my journey through life informed by Scripture, tradition, and reason.

When the picture on that television is the reality, who could ever want to even consider aborting that new beginning, stopping the development of that fertilized egg to fetus to finally delivered and welcomed child? No one.

The television picture is consistent with creation: a man and a woman wanting to extend the gift of life through the conception, nurture, birth, and care of another like themselves. It is part of God's creation intention, worthy of careful respect and deep reverence.

Real-Life Dramas of Unwanted Pregnancies

But there are other pictures not shown on television, save in dramas of the underbelly of life in fictional settings, where we can choose to write off the characterizations with shrugs or qualifications that keep the possibility of reality safely beyond arm's reach extended by the remote control. Consider these pictures:

- A young teenager, abused by her father or brother, sensing some mysterious change in her body, not sure what it is, and finally the realization—"I am pregnant."
- A young woman, engaged to be married in two months, raped at knifepoint, trying to forget as her body begins to tell her she will not forget, for it says to her, "You are pregnant."
- A forty-year-old single mother, already trying to care for six children, dependent on welfare and the support of a kind community around her, knows full well how the bonding takes place in her body once she begins to provide nourishment for a fetus, now finding that after another one-night stand it has happened again—"I am pregnant."
- A happily married couple with two adopted children, living out their desire to parent in the adoptive mode because they know pregnancy would surely cause the woman's death, practice birth control stringently but now find themselves confronted with a new truth—"We are pregnant anyway."

There are many pictures that could be drawn, many scenarios created, quite unlike that perfect picture on the television commercial. While we fervently hope it is the television scene that is most often played out in homes in our nation and around the world, we cannot ignore other pictures, other experiences. What do we do about them?

Very quickly we can turn to the issues of adopting children born to those who did not plan for them. It is a good option; many children and parents have enjoyed blessings beyond counting because of the option of adoption. And while the happy newly formed family, taking home that bundle of joy, coos and burbles, there is somewhere a woman, and perhaps a man, and perhaps another set of parents, who experience a loss and emptiness that will never be filled, no matter how wise the decision to release the child, how reasonable, how inescapable.

But, some say, abortion leaves the same emptiness. Perhaps, but not always, at least not the very same. There are many witnesses who tell stories of tearful relief and conviction that life never brought to fullness was the best for that potential child conceived under circumstances of anything but desire for new life.

Nevertheless, adoption must always be a thoroughly examined option for someone who does not want to bear a child but finds herself pregnant. The good fortune of such a child given to the care of those who wish for children and are unable to have them naturally is also a sign of God's generosity and grace. The abuses of those who broker adoptions should not turn us away from the potential of the choice as a way out of a terrible personal dilemma of unwanted pregnancy.

Ethical Grounds for Abortion

There is no ethical or moral room for casual decision for abortion. Promiscuity alone, discovery of having been in an illicit relationship, just not wanting the responsibility: Any reason in such a category is outside the bounds of what one who reveres life could consider as sufficient cause for the agonizing decision of abortion.

Yet, dare we say "never"? Dare we ever believe we can put ourselves in the skin of another person or set of persons and level judgment when the decision for abortion rises out of circumstances that hold no promise of sufficient life for the child that will be born? What if the pregnancy does irreparable physical or social damage to the one carrying the fetus? Or, what if the person carrying the fetus, or the fetus itself, faces a future endangered and without proper resources because of violence or another's deadly force?

Christian and Jewish faith traditions hold at their core the sacred nature of all living things, with special reverence and focus on the human creation. We share the notion of being created in the image of the first Creator, not physically to be sure, but in our being itself, the heart of thought and emotion and ability to think that sets us in unique relationship to the rest of God's precious creation. Therefore, discussion of abortion must always start with this remembrance of the holiness, the sacred nature, the God-likeness of human life. Such a starting point makes it very difficult to consider interruption of the development of life created in God's image. If one believes that image is at least foreseen in the fertilized egg, located in a nurturing womb, and beginning to surge with the urge that will become a full-blown God-image-carrying human, reverence for that holy potential is good and must be maintained.

No one should be left to the terror of this decision alone. It is about life, and ideally life is about community, and decisions about preventing the full development of life cry out for a community participation in the decision. In a perfect world, the decision to abort is the final and only resort left when all else is examined, weighed, pondered, and prayed through. What woman, regardless of age or status, dare face this dilemma alone? How can the weight of this terrible last choice of last resort be put on one pair of already burdened shoulders to bear alone?

It cannot. It must not be so. If there is to be a consideration of abortion, a community of persons of faith are needed to assist in ethical decision making. There must be those who love the pregnant woman: parents, friends, and husband or the one who has been part of impregnation (if he is in a caring relationship with the woman). There must be those who maintain some distance, while still linked in care: pastoral caregivers, physicians and nurses, and those who work with social situations surrounding the terror of this disturbing possibility. Conversation must be accompanied by careful thought and deep and earnest prayer. All alternatives must be explored, for this is potential life we are talking about, the very image of God.

But the one carrying that potential life is also made in the image of God, and also has a future to be considered. As surely as a newborn's environment is crucial to the future of that new life, so must the environment and future of the woman who is carrying the potential for that new life be considered. Not only must we ask, Is there a safe place, a nurturing place, a life-giving place for this soon-to-be-child? we must also ask, What will become of the woman now pregnant? Is she capable of healthfully caring the child to term? What permanent distress will be created in her life that will make her unable to care for the child appropriately, or to release its care to another without permanent damage to her? What will be the quality of life for this woman after the birth?

Living with Ambiguities, Not Absolutes

There are those who believe that life is composed of absolutes. For them there are some definitive realities that cannot be challenged or transgressed. It is a way of viewing life that is valid for those who hold it and provides for them a framework within which to live out their faith and life purposes.

There are others who, equally earnestly, believe that life is filled with ambiguities, with turning points that cannot be clearly, cleanly, without question predetermined. The direction to be taken at such junctures can only be discerned when at that juncture. All of the circumstances, possibilities, alternatives simply cannot be seen from afar or outside the immediate experience, or predicted. One thing is constant and unchanging for those who hold the latter view: God is. And within the "is" lies a deep pool of confidence that God is good, merciful, slow to anger, and of great compassion. Further, in that pool under "is" lies the abiding confidence of the "nowness" of God and involvement of God, especially at these critical turning points where the direction cannot be predetermined but must be prayed out, thought out, wrestled out, cried out, and pondered out at the time.

So it is that someone can approach the possibility of abortion with the confidence that God is present in that moment, present through their ability to reason, emote, gather information, pray, and be in community in decision making. And, most important, God has created us from the beginning to make such decisions. It is ours to do. We are both free to decide and have the responsibility to decide.

That freedom is terrifying. We have discovered secrets of the universe, all of God's making, that now make us able to consider life in ways never before a part of our human thought processes. Such discoveries are thrilling, liberating, and life giving, and demand of us careful, thoughtful, and prayerful work unknown to previous generations. The almost miraculous work of neonatal units that can sustain life for babies born much too soon is breath-taking. And in some cases, their work results in children with lifelong limitations. What to do? What does that say about how late one could justify an abortion as the removal of a fetus instead of a child?

Such knotty, difficult, heart-wrenching questions are not to be answered lightly. That we find ourselves, decades after *Roe v. Wade,* still experiencing heated arguments and, most terrifying and ungodly of all, violence against persons who reach decisions different from one's own, is but a sign of the impossibility of being very sure we know all there is to know about every situation that has arisen or will arise. It is a sign that we cannot be so audacious as to stand by an agonizing woman, appropriately struggling with prayer and counsel and all the other community wisdom I have suggested earlier, and dare to tell her she is wrong. Who can know that without having walked the journey to the decision with her? How audacious and judgmental and dangerous to our social soul, to say nothing of that soul for which all of us will be accountable to our Maker!

Yes, I believe there are extreme circumstances that may lead a woman and her surrounding community to make the terrible choice for abortion. Therefore I continue to insist that there be such a legal, safe, compassionate possibility for those rare circumstances. That others will abuse that provision is a devastating reality, but not so devastating as the removal of the provision altogether.

Let me share a story of contrasting experiences. One day I heard the report of a young married pregnant woman who had just heard the first fetal heartbeat and was ecstatic, and within hours I was with a weeping victim of a rape who had discovered she was pregnant. What a contrast! What a picture of real life—first beautiful, then tragic. I could not begin to fully comprehend either woman's emotions or potential future. But I could pray with both, and ponder with both, and be part of a surrounding community of discernment for both. For even that mother-to-be who heard that heartbeat had feelings of wonder and awe: Will I be adequate? Can we provide all a child will need? Will we be able to bear the dangers and risks of parenting as well as the joy? And the rape victim wondered, How can I look upon a child created out of fear and threat of life and find anything but a chain binding me to a night of terror and perhaps threatening my ability to ever freely love and generously nurture? How will I bear the time of maturation of this fetus, and what will it be like to know, though placed in a loving place, that this child was conceived in rage and danger?

Ah, the conundrums of human emotion, the extensiveness of human responsibility, the expansiveness of human knowledge, the remaining mysteries of personal knowing that belong to each individual that can never be fully known by another. When the agonizing decision is made for an abortion, after all the surrounding wisdom and guidance and prayer I have suggested, I pray there will be some gracious possibility that the woman will continue to be cared for gently. I pray she is spared the angry and ugly accusations and judgments of those who cannot possibly know her story. The story of one who seeks an abortion without such care and prayer, acting only for her own convenience, is quite different, and falls outside the circle of ethical and moral decision making.

We must take care whom we judge and whom we accuse lest we mistake the ethical, moral, agonized woman for the casual person who has seen pregnancy as an inconvenience only and knows how to take care of that. The latter is not the narrow doorway for which I advocate. But I do advocate that narrow doorway for the former, and I plead for mercy on the part of those who argue differently as they make their cases, remembering that in all cases we are talking about sacred human beings, made in the image of God. Even we who articulate different positions, even we are made in the image of God.

IS ABORTION EVER A LEGITIMATE MORAL CHOICE?

A *Response by* Sidney Callahan

Abortion on request is never a legitimate moral choice, although in the United States our laws now permit such abortions. Unfortunately, at this point we live in a society where medical technology is routinely used to destroy developing human life in the womb. As we accept the procedure of routine abortion we are damaging cultural values that protect our moral commitments to one another.

Western society has long affirmed the principle that no human life should be disposed of as property, or used as a means to another's end. This ban against unilateral acts of killing has been validated over and over. Whether one agrees with the biblical commandment "Thou shall not kill," or follows the rule never to do to another what you would not have done to you, no one has been given the right to arbitrarily take away the life and future potential of another. No matter what the temptation, the life of other human beings must be held safe from harm.

But abortion performed at the request of a woman extinguishes human life and violates the moral demand for equal and just treatment for all members of humanity. When we take away the legal and moral protection of vulnerable human lives in the womb, we endorse a logic of domination and expediency; the strong dominate the weak, as in the marketplace or in the jungle. Dependent human lives are discounted despite the fact that in the interdependent human life cycle, each of us will be dependent for 20 percent of our existence.

Factors at Work to Justify Abortion

How has this situation come about? Many factors are at work. While everyone recognizes that fetal life is human life, it is considered too undeveloped to count as equal to ourselves. Tiny embryos at the beginning of their existence do not look like babies, so it seems less immoral or upsetting to kill them. All the same we know from science that if we could replay the movie of every person's life backward, we would arrive at that embryonic being that contains the genetic information and dynamic program that makes us possible. The growth of technologies such as ultrasound imagery now allow us to see into the womb and observe the heartbeats of each new life. An embryo is a being on the way to becoming a being like us.

Yet women have been assured that it is their moral and legal right to interrupt the life that has begun, and to extinguish the life of the fetus. The justification has been that women must have the liberty to exercise control over their bodies even at the cost of killing. Some abortion advocates believe only early abortions should be permitted, but many pro-choice advocates will go so far as to defend women's right to late abortions. These late abortions are recognized to be hardly different from infanticide, but they are still accepted as a woman's right.

I think we can understand the prevalence of abortion and the approval of late abortions as a lingering manifestation of the entrenched human practice of infanticide. Infanticide as a custom has never been thoroughly rejected by our culture. In much of Western history, despite Christian disapproval, babies were exposed or given away or allowed to die when families decided it was necessary. Indeed, many human groups have had a long tradition of accepting infanticide. From an evolutionary biological perspective, it is efficient for parents to invest only in those offspring that will have the best chances for survival. In earlier cultures it was the father who decided whether the child lived or died. Now we let women make the decision. Either way, the new life, born or unborn, is still thought of as the property of the parents and seen to serve their reproductive purposes.

Women and Decision Making

Today, many women procuring abortions do so not only for themselves but on behalf of their present families or the future children they will have with different partners or in better circumstances. They are exercising control over their bodies but are also controlling the formation of their family. They will have children when and with whom they choose. Often they see the abortion as a form of mercy-killing that will serve the welfare of their existing or future children, and help them out of a trying situation.

Unfortunately, with the growth of medical technology, abortion offers a quick solution to a problem pregnancy. The procedure can be over in a few hours. On the other hand, it takes energy and effort to effect a nonviolent nurturing solution that avoids killing. Having a child and offering that child for adoption is painful, so women opt to abort instead. Having and rearing the child seems an enormous undertaking. Often women decide to abort during a period of great stress. A woman may be poor, unemployed, and without the support of her partner.

Since abortion has become institutionalized as a routine individualized option, women have lost their moral right to hold men responsible for the support of the offspring they engender. When I worked at a pregnancy care center, we often saw young women threatened with abandonment by their boyfriends (and sometimes by their families) if they did not abort the pregnancy. A modern young man can feel responsible only to provide money for the abortion, or perhaps only half the fee. So many persons in the society accept and recommend abortion that it becomes difficult for a woman to choose to carry her child. Despite the wide network of pregnancy care centers, there are still far too few social supports for women with problem pregnancies.

Amidst such social conditions are many repeat abortions; they serve as a backup for contraception. Repeat abortions are more likely to have dangerous psychological and physical consequences. We do not yet know the long-term effects of abortion on women, but certainly for many women the experience produces negative consequences. Few relationships between men and women survive an abortion unscathed. Many young women find themselves exploited and unsupported, all in the name of sexual and reproductive liberty.

Permissive Abortion Morally Invalid

The acceptance of permissive abortion validates a narrow view of moral obligation. A woman, and increasingly a man, is told that if he or she did not plan the pregnancy, then the fetus has no moral claim. Only informed consent and an explicit contract to reproduce creates a moral obligation to support a pregnancy. This idea that moral obligations only arise from individual consent and contract is dangerous to life in the community.

After all, no one consents to or chooses the parents or families or neighbors they live with, yet they have moral obligations to them. For that matter, no one plans to be a member of Earth's ecosystem, but we have obligations to take care of the environment. If we are in an auto accident with strangers, we have obligations not to walk away from them. And an accidental pregnancy does not involve strangers, but instead one's own offspring with kinship obligations. The idea that the reality of a fetal life does not exist unless a woman grants it reality and human status sets a dangerous moral precedent. Reality is not reversible at will.

Yes, human beings must exercise control and planning for the future, but unexpected emergencies can always arise in which we must help those who need us. A fetal life has no life support other than a womb for the nine months it takes for birth. Only women have the biological and procreative power to save and nurture new lives. The power to meet this need, and the desperateness of the need impel the moral obligation of women to offer nurturance. It is also the case that all family relationships are built on unconditional acceptance of needs of family members. If we validate the right to reject and destroy our offspring at the outset of life, it becomes harder to give children the kind of acceptance they need. Sex selection and the search for the perfect child grow out of the right of abortion on request. Children become products of their parents' will rather than accepted as gifts with their own inalienable rights to life. The ready acceptance of abortion corrupts the relationships between men and women and the parent-child relationship.

Are there any exceptions or cases in which abortion is morally acceptable? Yes, no right is ever absolute in all circumstances. A fundamental human right, however, can only be overridden for a moral cause and not just expediency. Such a condition would be met when one effects some greater claim of justice that also supports the original right overridden. Thus a woman too has a fundamental right to life, and medical abortions to save her life or health in emergencies would morally exemplify the basic human right to life. In cases of rape and incest, however, the new life in question is not physically endangering its mother and has done nothing wrong. A woman may not be able to raise such a child successfully, but she still should not choose to kill her own offspring.

The Morality of Pro-Life Versus Abortion

Many fundamental considerations and assumptions will influence judgments on the morality of abortion. First, there will be the valuation of life itself. When faced with a new life or an involuntary pregnancy, there is a world of difference in whether one first asks, Why continue? or Why not? Where is the burden of proof going to rest? The concept of "compulsory pregnancy" is as distorted as labeling life "compulsory aging." Also, how is a woman's pregnancy viewed? If pregnancy is seen as a pathological medical condition that seriously disables a woman, then it will always be viewed as a burden. If, on the other hand, pregnancy is seen as a process that evolutionary selection has made normal for women and the species, then pregnancy is not a disease. In my judgment, medical progress has made modern pregnancies relatively safe, so that women are able to work and function normally while pregnant. The pain of childbirth has also been tamed by drugs.

The value and place of children in women's lives is also an issue that affects the abortion debate. No woman should have to have children to validate her femininity. But many observers have noted that while having children makes a young woman's life more difficult, having had children helps the lives of older women. Older women flourish in extended families and benefit from the care of children in their old age. The difficult time in women's lives is during their youthful reproductive years when childbearing and work are in conflict.

Thus, those who wish to help women avoid abortion must try to improve women's lives when they are young.

117

Adolescent girls must be empowered in ways that do not make them dependent on male approval or conform to male's sexuality and lifestyles. Young women need career goals and access to education and health care. If women are to be truly liberated, and thereby become able to choose to nurture their children, they must have access to work and child care. Health care for women and children must be available, as they are in other industrialized countries.

Those of us in the pro-life movement can have hope. It has taken generations for women to be granted equality and full dignity. It may take more decades before we see that the fate of fetal life is entwined with our own moral well-being.

CHAPTER SIX

IS ABORTING A "PROBLEMATIC" FETUS ETHICALLY ACCEPTABLE?

Overview

P articularly perplexing is the moral question of whether aborting a "problematic" fetus can be deemed ethically acceptable. Decisions to abort or not to abort are made daily, based on anticipated disabilities and diseases. Since the issue has become both ethically and politically sensitive, and subject to great misunderstandings and misinterpretations, the question often goes unexplored and undiscussed.

Judy C. Martz and Harvey C. Martz, whose beloved son has Down syndrome, acknowledge with some reluctance that "there are times and situations when it is ethically justifiable to terminate pregnancy because there are significant genetic problems." But they insist that the morality depends on following three critical steps in decision making. First, current medical information must be obtained so that the couple can differentiate between different disabilities or genetic defects. Not every type justifies abortion, and the quest to produce only "near perfect" babies reflects immorality. Consultation with spiritual advisors and with parents of children suffering the same condition are also deemed essential. The Martzes describe a fetus as a potential person deserving respect, but who is not equal to a full-term infant. Believing that God does not will disabilities, and that the life and world are not perfect, they are convinced God will be supportive of conscientious persons who choose to abort.

Duke University ethicists Stanley Hauerwas and Joel Shuman question the term "problematic," contending that all children—in fact all human beings—are in some sense "problematic." They choose to illustrate "the fundamentally arbitrary nature of distinguishing those disabilities that justify abortion from those that do not." They deplore thinking that suggests "a certain kind of disabled life is a life not worth living." If the same children are placed in a L'Arche home, living in Christian community with the able-bodied, their lives "once again appear to be worth living." Hauerwas and Shuman challenge the ethics of measuring children by whether they are economically productive. Christian baptism reminds us that our children are not our own, but a gift of God to be received. Christians should not think of abortion as a "personal choice" nor even ask whether aborting a problematic fetus seems appropriate for the Christian community.

IS ABORTING A "PROBLEMATIC" FETUS ETHICALLY ACCEPTABLE?

A Response by Judy C. Martz and Harvey C. Martz

Amber and Mike, a married couple in their midtwenties, experienced pregnancy for the first time. During a routine ultrasound examination around the twentieth week of pregnancy, their physician discerned some significant problems. The fetus had neither arms nor legs. A level-two ultrasound test, an amniocentesis, and a consultation with a geneticist led to the diagnosis of a "pseudo thalidomide" fetus. The couple was informed that their son seemed to have no rib cage or lungs, and probably would not survive birth.

Active in their church, the couple told fellow church members and pastors what they were facing and asked for prayer and support during the time they were deciding whether to terminate the pregnancy. They talked with their friends at church about what would be the right thing to do.

Friends who were vehemently opposed to abortion encouraged the couple to continue with the pregnancy and to wait for a miracle from God that would restore the fetus to normalcy. Their obstetrician told them that if the fetus died *in utero,* there could be a chance of a very serious infection for the mother. After asking God for direction, the couple ultimately decided to terminate the pregnancy at about the twenty-second week.

Since medical testing during a pregnancy now can

reveal problems and possibilities for the future life of a child, the knowledge from that testing is creating new ethical dilemmas. We believe there are times and situations when it is ethically justifiable to terminate a pregnancy because there are significant genetic problems, but only when the following steps are part of that decision by the parent or parents.

Steps Toward a Decision

First, the parent or parents should obtain current medical information about the likely level of health and disability, and about the quality of future life for the child. Parents should be encouraged to talk with more than one health professional about the issues and to do everything possible to be sure that the data and advice they are receiving are up-to-date.

The possible range of quality and style of life varies widely with different disabilities or genetic conditions. The decision of the couple at the beginning of this essay was clearer for them because they had been advised that there was probably no chance for their child to be alive after birth. If there had been some chance, they said that they would probably have continued the pregnancy and that they were not frightened by the prospect of being parents of a child with special needs.[1]

There are other genetic conditions that also offer a clearer decision to abort, because the chance for survival is not good or because the problems after birth can be so enormous. Such diagnoses are anencephaly, Tay-Sachs, Hunter syndrome, and other conditions that could lead to death or degeneration within the first few months of life.

But there is a range of other conditions in which many people, after scientific research, prayer, and ethical reflection, choose to continue the pregnancy and give birth. These include spina bifida, muscular dystrophy, cystic fibrosis, and Down syndrome.[2] Potential parents need to receive current medical advice about what is possible for children with these disabilities, because there has been much medical progress in recent years about the life quality for children with these disabilities. Simultaneously, in the U.S. there has been much progress in accepting and assisting the approximately 10 percent of people who have some kind of disability. At least one placement agency, for example, reports a waiting list for families who want to adopt an infant with Down syndrome.

Second, the potential parent or parents should consult with other parents of children with the same condition, so that they may learn from those families' personal experiences. These experiences will vary, depending on the severity of the disability. Even within a particular disability, such as Down syndrome, there is a wide expanse of ability level. The pregnant couple needs to ask other parents to be forthright about the stresses and joys that can be involved in having a family member with a serious disability. The stresses are real, and some families are not able to cope effectively with the emotional and physical demands that are required.

A third step for potential parents involves consultation with their minister, rabbi, or spiritual counselor about their understanding of life and birth, and ethics. The theological assumptions people bring to this kind of decision are critically important. For instance, we believe that a fetus is not just a mass of tissue but instead is a potential human being. However, a fetus at twenty-two weeks is, in our theology, a potential human being and does not have the same importance as born persons.

Theological Assumptions

One fundamental theological question revolves around the question of when does life begin? The story of creation in the

123

second chapter of Genesis declares, that when God breathes into the man the breath of life, the man becomes a "nefesh," a "living being" (Genesis 2:7). This means that without the breath of life, God's wondrous human creation in Genesis was still a potential person. While respecting the potential life that the pregnant mother and father are deliberating about, we do not grant the same importance to a twenty-two-week fetus as to a full-term infant. If the parents believe that the claims of the fetus are equal to their own claims, they will have great difficulty in terminating the pregnancy no matter how profound the genetic abnormalities may be. However, the joys are real also, and many families, including the authors, report richly satisfying family lives.

Another theological assumption that will be important to explore regards an understanding of the will of God. It is not our belief that God wills children to have cystic fibrosis or spina bifida or Hunter syndrome or other disabilities. God is at work for good in the events of life (Romans 8:28-30), but God acts not like a cosmic puppeteer who chooses some folks to have certain disabilities and others to be relatively free of disabilities.

We have experienced much superficial God-talk around disability issues. Some people may say to a pregnant couple that God has chosen them specifically to be parents of a child with special needs, unaware of how cruel this notion is of a God who wants some children to be disabled, or unaware of the fact that some families break up when confronted with the ongoing demands that some disabilities can bring.

Third, from a theological perspective, life and the world are not perfect. Random things and events do occur in our world. Jesus seems to support this notion of randomness when he talks about a tower that falls on people by accident in Luke 13:4. Accidents, even genetic accidents, do happen, but God's intent for creation remains wholeness and wellness.

This means that the people who are doing genetic research that will lead to fewer genetic conditions are on God's side and are doing God's work. The ministry of Jesus, which includes healing people with disabilities, also represents part of God's will for humanity. In the fourth chapter of Matthew's Gospel, the writer portrays Jesus as beginning his ministry in Galilee by doing three things: teaching, preaching, and healing (Matthew 4:23). In the Gospel of Mark, by the end of the first chapter, Jesus has already healed persons with convulsions, epilepsy, and leprosy. Yes, God's intent for God's creation is wholeness and wellness.

However, if a couple facing a problematic pregnancy believe there are no accidents or coincidence—that everything that occurs happens because God wills it—then they will have more difficulty seeing the option of terminating the pregnancy, even if there are profound and life-threatening problems. They may believe that God has chosen the child to have a disability, and to think about terminating the pregnancy would be to act against God's will. Other conscientious persons of faith may determine that God never wills such extreme disabilities, and therefore abortion is theologically and ethically justifiable and necessary.

Risks of Justifying Termination of Pregnancy

There are some risks in affirming the moral justification of terminating a pregnancy where there is a problematic fetus. First, some people might misuse this position to further the notion that only "near perfect" people should be born. We unequivocally reject that belief. A person's disability is only one descriptor of that person's whole being, and it may be a much less significant descriptor than other characteristics. Musician Stevie Wonder is a gifted composer and performer who happens to be blind. People know him more for his music than for his disability.

We also lift up other lesser-known persons who have

made no well-publicized contributions to human culture, but whose enthusiasm for life and unabashed love and acceptance of their friends and family continue to be inspiring and prompt others to cherish companionship and close relationships with them.

All persons can contribute positively to life. Amber and Mike, the couple mentioned previously, told of some friends who learned that the baby they were carrying had a condition known as trisomy 18, a syndrome characterized by serious physical disorders and mental retardation. The friends chose to continue the pregnancy and deliver at full term. While their baby lived only three days, they told of the positive way in which the child had affected their lives.

Second, our position could be misused if people fail to do their homework well in meeting with several health care professionals and with families who have children with special needs, learning what might be possible for the child the potential parents are carrying. Twenty years ago, some physicians were still encouraging parents of newborns with moderate disabilities to place the children in institutions and not even bring them home from the hospital. Potential parents are urged to be aggressive in learning about what is possible for children with special needs, to like the child they are carrying, and to be able to make an informed decision instead of one based on outdated information.

Our own experience of a son with Down syndrome (now in his midtwenties) has led us to see how rich and full the lives of persons with his disability and other disabilities can be in today's culture. Our son Todd works on a college campus, is a member of a fraternity, and lives with fraternity brothers, though he has significant needs, requires much support, and is not an enrolled student at the college. His college student friends and others tell us that their lives are enriched by knowing him, and by their friendship with him.

A third risk emerges when parents fail to do the prayerful, theological, and ethical wrestling that is crucial, but instead make a choice that is glib, facile, and based on what is immediately convenient for them. While we fully support the decision Amber and Mike made, part of our support is because of the intense process they went through to make their decision. They prayed, sought information from several physicians, gained counsel from church friends and pastors, and demonstrated respect for the potential life that they had created. Additionally, they shared with other people the personal and ethical dilemma and decision they were facing, asking for their prayers.

Doing Grief Work

After terminating the pregnancy and permitting an early delivery, Amber and Mike had the body cremated, held a memorial service, and scattered the ashes in the church yard. A garden was planted on Caleb's due date as another reminder of him. They consistently referred to him by name as soon as they knew they were carrying a boy. And they have done and are doing the grief work that people need to do even when there has not been a live birth. These parents experienced the loss of a child that they were eagerly anticipating from the beginning of the pregnancy. Though they never knew Caleb as a developed and fully formed person, their grief was real, necessary, and appropriate.[3]

Similar types of grief work appear imperative when parents give birth to a child with a disability, because they will grieve the loss of a child they were anticipating and will then need to adjust and create new hopes and dreams for the child they have.

The adjustment of parenting a child with special needs will mean that the family will usually go through the typical journey of grieving, which can involve denial, anger, numbness, depression, and acceptance. This grief is expectable and involves the loss of the original dream or hope or anticipated future, and the replacement of that hope with a different anticipated future.[4]

In Conclusion

Making a moral decision whether to abort a problematic fetus necessitates thoughtful and responsible attention to the various dilemmas and dimensions of decision making. We cannot say in advance what conditions warrant whether abortion is justified or not. The parents/mother alone have to make that choice. We believe that if the parent(s) do the homework outlined, they will be the ethical expert(s) about what is morally possible and responsible for them. But if a couple or a single parent follows conscientiously and prayerfully the steps we have cited, the decision they make will be good and right, and God will be supportive.

NOTES

1. In one family where a child was born with hemophilia, the father left the family after a few years because he was unable to cope with the additional emotional and physical stresses of being a parent of a child with this medical need. The mother remarried, and the son, now an adult, has a responsible job as a bookkeeper in a large automobile dealership.

2. For portions of this differentiation of conditions we are indebted to bioethicist Adrienne Arch's article, "Real Moral Dilemmas," *Christianity and Crisis,* 14 July 1986, p. 239.

3. Two booklets for consultation would be *A Guide to Resources in Perinatal Bereavement* (Washington, D.C.: National Center for Education in Maternal and Child Health, 1988); and *A Workbook for Pastoral Care of Individuals and Families with Special Needs* (Washington, D.C.: National Center for Education in Maternal and Child Health, 1988), comp. and ed. Robert C. Baumiller, with assistance of John Fletcher and Lawrence Madden.

4. "Loss and Grief Cycle," a pamphlet by Dr. Gil Foley, Family Centered Resource Center, Reading, Pennsylvania.

IS ABORTING A "PROBLEMATIC" FETUS ETHICALLY ACCEPTABLE?

A Response by Stanley Hauerwas and Joel Shuman

The question, Is abortion of a "problematic" fetus ethically acceptable? serves as a nice example to support the contention that for questions of ethics, description—and not decision—is what really matters. That is why the first thing that occurs to us when we are asked whether it is morally permissible to abort a problematic fetus is how this way of putting the matter is dependent on a politics whose presuppositions are from a theological perspective themselves "problematic." Thus we can only begin discussing this matter by asking, Problematic in what sense, and for whom?

Consider, for example, what the adjective "problematic" does in a question about the permissibility of abortion. Anyone who has children is likely to agree that the children are all in some sense "problematic." In spite of their relative innocence and the great joy, they frequently bring to those of us privileged to have them in our lives, raising children is a difficult, costly, and time-consuming business. Moreover, like their parents, children are born the broken citizens of a broken creation, who inevitably do things or have things happen to them that cause both them and their families considerable anguish. In this sense, we are all problematic.

If all of us are from birth really problematic, what kinds of differences make a fetus sufficiently problematic to abort? Moreover, who should be permitted to decide who is problematic or not? By raising these matters we do not wish to trivialize the considerable challenges associated with parenting children with significant mental or physical disabilities; we wish, rather, to illustrate the fundamentally arbitrary nature of distinguishing those disabilities that justify abortion from those that do not.[1] In our culture we presume such decisions are "private" ones to be made by parents of good conscience in consultation with their physician; what we do not see is the way that presumption is illustrative—not to mention constitutive—of our profound isolation from one another. Because we are more or less strangers who cannot imagine what it might mean to share one another's lives, we feign understanding when parents abort a disabled fetus because they feel they have no other choice.

The overriding sentiment toward children with those disabilities that seem to justify their being singled out as "problematic" is that "it would be better had they never been born." Once such a sentiment has been expressed it serves as a tacit justification for aborting these children; for once we can agree that a certain kind of disabled life is a life not worth living, then we can find no reason to proscribe not permitting those lives not to exist in the first place.

Yet often the problem with assumptions of this sort is that they are based on a definition of "problematic" that depends more on our unwillingness to create human spaces for disabled children than on the children's disabilities per se. For example, if someone enters a "day room" in an institution for disabled children and finds the smell of urine and feces strong, some of the children prone to violent self-stimulation, others partly or fully undressed, that person's normal reaction is likely to be disgust. Seeing such a scene, one cannot help thinking, "These children would be better off dead." But if the same children are placed in a L'Arche home, where persons with disabilities live together in Christian community with the able-bodied, they suddenly become human and their lives once again appear to be worth living. Those who assert that some abortions are justifiable because some lives are not worth living most often make that assertion in the name of compassion. The assumption is that persons with disabilities suffer in ways that the rest of us do not; consequently, aborting a fetus with a disability becomes a way to prevent suffering. Who would dare argue that the prevention of suffering is not a good thing? We have no doubt that the disabled do suffer, and often in horrible ways. Yet we fear that those who sanction the abortion of disabled fetuses in the name of compassion are in fact unaware of the subtle ways what they call compassion is in fact a mask for the politics of democratic capitalism and the ways that politics—rather than the politics of the church—shapes our understanding of what it means to live a good life.[2]

A capitalist political economy like the one in which we live requires for its ongoing success a cadre of disciplined, talented bodies who participate willingly and vigorously in the cycle of production and consumption in their own self-interest. In fact, one of the principal means by which we judge ourselves and others in our society *capable* of living well is by projecting our capacity to work, meaning, in this case, to earn and to spend. We define ourselves in this culture by what we do or produce, by how much we earn, and by how much we own. Thus, from the perspective of a capitalist political economy, children with disabilities are indeed problematic, in that their lives subvert all of our standard accounts of normal, successful life.

There is a sense here in which we are merely belaboring the obvious. All children, as we mention above, are costly, in terms of both time and money. And this is especially true of children with disabilities, whose care can very easily destroy their families financially. What is not so obvious, however, is the profound sense in which our political economy pushes us to commodify every aspect of our lives, to such an extent that we begin to see even our children in this way. Thus we understand them not as gifts, but as investments that are purely the products of our own labor.

Such an account of child rearing puts significant pressure on parents to produce only "normal" children who will be happy, healthy, and above all successful, which is to say economically productive. This is an outcome that is unlikely, if not impossible, in the case of children with significant disabilities. In light of these considerations, it is no wonder that parents who discover their unborn child is "problematic" feel a considerable burden to abort. Apart from a different kind of society whose practices make possible concrete alternatives, warehousing or financial ruin may well be the only alternatives to abortion.[3]

We are thinking here of the church and its practices, particularly baptism, which we believe makes possible a radically different way of thinking about ourselves and our children. Baptism, by making our bodies part of the one Body of Christ, subverts the normative status given to the contemporary nuclear family and the productive consumer, and offers alternative accounts of what it means to be a normal member of a typical family. In baptism, we are reminded that our lives and the lives of our children are not our own, but gifts from God to be received as such.[4]

The plainly political language of the baptismal liturgy indicates how the sacrament might affect the way we think about our obligation to "problematic" children. Christian parents who bring their children to be baptized acknowledge by their promise to keep their children "under the ministry and guidance of the Church" their relinquishment of control over their children's lives.[5] The practice of baptism thus frees parents from the tyranny of having to decide for themselves what to do in the case of a "problematic" pregnancy; for by virtue of their own baptism and the prospect of the baptism of their child, they are made part of a community possessing the capacity for rightly discerning how best to care for such a child.[6]

Articulating a response to the question of what to do with a problematic fetus through the lens of baptism not only reconstitutes our understanding about who has the authority to make such decisions, it also reconfigures the way we understand who is responsible for the care of such children. The child's parents, in other words, are not the only ones making promises as part of the liturgy. By pledging to surround the children being baptized, with a community of loving care, members of the congregation are promising to make themselves and their resources available to the children and their parents.[7] This is simply another way in which the community of the baptized is a community in which those who "seem to be weaker are indispensable," and in which all the members "may have the same care for one another."[8]

It is one thing to point out ways the baptismal liturgy might help us imagine ways of caring for, rather than aborting, problematic children, and another thing altogether to put those alternatives into practice. The church is, as the author of 1 Peter puts it, a community of "aliens and exiles" in this world, a people involved in a continual struggle to embody in their own time and place the identity given them through baptism. Such a struggle is particularly difficult in the culture in which we find ourselves, a culture based on the presumption that when everything is said and done, we are our own creators.

In the final analysis, our world turns out to be not so different from the town of Feliciana, the small Louisiana village that is the setting for Walker Percy's novel *The Thanatos Syndrome.* In Feliciana, the powers-that-be are involved in a grand, horrific scheme to produce a brilliant, efficient, and altogether happy citizenry that is completely devoid of moral imagination. Coincident with their sinister efforts to chemically improve the lot of the average citizen is their participation in the widespread euthanizing of the elderly and the disabled, and the abortion of problematic fetuses, all in the name of "tenderness." In the book's closing scene, one of the protagonists, an insane old priest named Father Smith, confronts these "Qualitarians" at a Mass in the hospital chapel by proclaiming that the tenderness in whose name they have done their work is in fact a great evil that "leads to the gas chambers," the indiscriminate killing of anyone who does not fit their narrow definition of what is normal. He exhorts them as he concludes his homily:

> Please do this one favor for me, dear doctors. If you have a patient, young or old, suffering dying, afflicted, useless, born or unborn, whom you for the best of reasons wish to put out of his misery—I beg only one thing of you, dear doctors! Please send him to us. Don't kill them! We'll take them—all of them! Please send them to us! I swear to you you won't be sorry. We will all be happy about it! I promise you, and I know that you believe me, that we will take care of him, her—we will even call on you to help us take care of them!—and you will not have to make such a decision. God will bless you for it and you will offend no one except the great Prince Satan, who rules the world. That is all.[9]

Whether Father Smith might have been thinking of the Sacrament of Baptism when he made this proclamation is, of course, absolutely speculative. What is less a matter of speculation is that one of the great challenges confronting the church in this day is whether we will live into our baptisms such that we are a community that says of the problematic: "Please send them to us!" Until we can answer that question in the affirmative, we bear the burden of responsibility for those parents who feel they have no choice but to abort a disabled child.

We are aware that many will respond to our argument by saying that this is the very problem, that "yours may be a worthy ideal, but it's just not the way the world is. In fact, these are matters of personal choice." Such a response, however, is just a reminder that, as we suggested above, the question of whether to abort a problematic fetus has its origins in a politics other than the politics of the church. The very idea that the question of what is to be done with such a child is a matter of "personal choice" is itself counter to the politics of baptism. Thus the question is not whether the abortion of a problematic fetus is ethically acceptable—a question that presupposes something called ethics that is independent of politics—but rather what has happened that Christians have come to believe such a question is the right one to ask.

NOTES

1. See, for example, Hauerwas's account of the debate between Drs. Lorber and Freeman over whether children born with meningomylocele manifesta should receive treatment or be permitted to die. "Selecting Children to Live or Die: An Ethical Analysis of the Debate Between Dr. Lorber and Dr. Freeman on the Treatment of Meningomylocele," in *Death, Dying, and Euthanasia*, eds. Dennis Horan and David Hall (Washington, D.C.: University Publications of America, 1977), pp. 228-49.

2. When we juxtapose "the politics of the church" and "the politics of democratic capitalism," we are referring not to those debates in the wider American culture between right and left, but to the distinction between that communal way of life inaugurated in the life, death, and resurrection of Jesus, and the way of life characteristic of contemporary American society right and left. Here we are influenced to a significant extent by John Howard Yoder's important book *The Politics of Jesus* (Grand Rapids, Mich.: Eerdmans, 1972).

THE BEFUDDLED STORK

3. Our thinking here is dependent to a significant extent on John Milbank's article, "Socialism of the Gift, Socialism by Grace," in *New Blackfriars* 77/910 (December 1996): 535. Milbank argues that capitalism "precludes community. This is because (let us remind ourselves), it makes the prime purpose of society as a whole and also of individuals to be one of accumulation of abstract wealth, or of power-to-do-things in general, and rigorously subordinates any desire to do anything concrete in particular, including the formation of social relationships."

4. Consider the introduction to one of the services of baptism found in *The United Methodist Book of Worship* (Nashville: The United Methodist Publishing House, 1993), p. 95, where the minister says to the congregation, "Brothers and sisters in Christ: Through the Sacrament of Baptism we are initiated into Christ's holy Church. We are incorporated into God's mighty acts of salvation and given new birth through water and the Spirit. All this is God's gift, offered to us without price."

5. Ibid., p. 104.

6. For an account of the politics of such a community, see John Howard Yoder, "The Hermeneutics of Peoplehood," in *The Priestly Kingdom* (Notre Dame: University of Notre Dame Press, 1984), pp. 15-45.

7. Baptismal Covenant, *The United Methodist Book of Worship*, pp. 104-5.

8. 1 Corinthians 12:22, 25.

9. Walker Percy, *The Thanatos Syndrome* (New York: Fawcett Columbine, 1987), p. 361.

CHAPTER SEVEN

CAN "PARTIAL-BIRTH" ABORTION BE A LEGITIMATE MORAL CHOICE?

Overview

I n the United States, abortion has evolved into an explosive political debate. Every candidate for major public office and every potential Supreme Court justice must face a litmus test on their personal and public policy views regarding abortion. In recent years the most hotly contested disagreements have focused on policy questions of whether late-term (partial-birth) abortions can be legitimate moral choices. The medical procedure called "intact dilation and extraction" (D&X) has been especially controversial.

Tex S. Sample examines the dilemma of a couple facing a late-term abortion prompted by concerns for the mother's mental health amid current "political machinations" that seek to take decisions away from the woman and attending physician. Personally against D&X and late-term abortions, Sample struggles with the question of making exceptions to his own disposition by examining the Bible. Among the passages explored is Numbers 5:11-31, which he concludes is "the only instance of an 'abortion' in Scripture, and it is caused by God." He concludes that neither Scripture nor church tradition are very helpful to persons struggling to make a decision about abortion. Rejecting situational ethics, and pointing to the reign of God in the Christian community, Sample affirms a virtue of hospitality. "To insist that a women be hospitable when she herself needs shelter is hardly a Kingdom virtue." If the threatened mental health of a mother means she cannot be hospitable to the fetus, then, tragically, a late-term abortion is ethically justifiable.

Joan Burgess Winfrey, self-described as an evangelical, pro-life feminist, emphasizes biblical understandings that underscore the sanctity of life in the image of God, and reverence for life. Declaring partial-birth abortions as both immoral and unchristian, she deplores a culture unwilling to care for "unwanted children" and others who are regarded as "high maintenance." She believes that discussion of partial-birth abortions has revealed "the rationalizations and euphemisms that have undergirded abortion on demand." Recent advances in perinatology (particularly the care of fetuses born not fully developed) have dramatically enhanced the survivability of premature babies, undercutting arguments of abortion advocates. *Roe v. Wade* is compared to the *Dred Scott* decision of 1857, the latter determining African Americans were not persons, and the former denying "personhood to an unborn child." She does acknowledge that no obstetrician "would elect to place a mother's life in extreme jeopardy to sustain a fetus without the mother's consent." Maternal mortality, she contends, is extremely rare, while the use of abortions, including late-term, is shockingly high.

CAN "PARTIAL-BIRTH" ABORTION BE A LEGITIMATE MORAL CHOICE?

A *Response by* Tex S. Sample

Sue is twenty-four weeks pregnant. She and her husband, Jim, want this child very much. They are deeply concerned, however, about Sue's struggle with chronic depression, which she has suffered off and on throughout her adult life. The pregnancy triggered a deepening problem. During the third month of the pregnancy she began to have serious thoughts about suicide, and late in her fifth month she took an overdose of sleeping pills, an act that she regarded as "accidental," that is, as something she did not intend, but that she cannot explain. Her physician believes that she needs an abortion for the sake of her mental health and that she must give thorough attention to her depression before taking on another pregnancy.

Since the abortion will be late-term, the doctor wants to do an intact dilation and extraction. He explains the procedure in graphic terms: It begins with the turning of the fetus in a feet-first position, followed by pulling all of the body of the fetus, except the head, from the womb. The procedure then requires the physician to puncture the skull of the fetus, to insert a tube in this puncture, and to suction the contents of the fetus's head sufficiently to make vaginal delivery of the fetus possible.

Sue and Jim both recoil at how gruesome the procedure is. Why would it ever be used? The physician answers that it is typically used when a fetus is dead or has major malformations of the fetus, or when the life and health of the pregnant woman are at stake. In this case, he is deeply concerned about Sue's mental health, and the consequences of continuing this pregnancy. This is the best procedure for her under these circumstances.

Are not other procedures available? Could not labor be induced with drugs? The cervix, he says, is very resistant to dilation until around thirty-six weeks. Drug-induced labor takes two to four days, is very painful, and runs the risk of uterine rupture, which is potentially very dangerous.

What about a cesarean section? It usually involves twice as much blood loss, for one thing. More than that, prior to thirty-four weeks the thickness of the uterus will not allow the usual horizontal incision, requiring instead a vertical one. While any incision in the uterus poses difficulties for future pregnancy, a vertical incision puts at risk Sue's health and jeopardizes a future pregnancy, which would require yet another cesarean. The doctor reiterates that the D&X procedure is the safest and best option in her case.[1]

The issue of late-term abortion is hotly contested. In what follows here, I make the case for such abortions under exceptional circumstances that include the mental health of the pregnant woman. I examine this in relation to two issues. The first has to do with national social policy. The second concerns a Christian argument that makes late-term abortion a permissible act.

Social Policy, Politics, and Abortion

The circumstance faced by Sue and Jim goes to the heart of the national debate about late-term abortion. This debate does not focus on D&X to save the pregnant woman's life; most sides of the debate grant this exception. Rather, the issue focuses on whether the health, and especially the mental health, of the pregnant woman is a permissible exception. A review of court rulings and legislation will clarify this issue.

In 1995, Congress was brought the first "partial-birth abortion ban" bill making it a federal crime to perform a D&X abortion. The only exceptions were that the abortion is required to save the life of the pregnant woman and that no other procedure will suffice for this purpose.[2]

This bill was vetoed by President Clinton because he wanted the exception of "serious, adverse health consequences to the mother" within the bill's provisions. Here, Clinton is clearly on solid Constitutional grounds, because the Supreme Court has consistently ruled since *Roe v. Wade* in 1973 that the health of the pregnant woman is one exception to the state's right to regulate and prohibit abortions after the time of fetal viability.[3] The Congress was not able to override Clinton's veto, but doubtless such legislation will be reintroduced in the Congress in subsequent legislative sessions.

Without an exception of the woman's physical and mental health, such legislation places Congress in the role of the physician, the pregnant woman, and her family. It denies the medical expertise of the physician in the care of her/his patients and overrides the claim of the woman and her family to attend to issues of her own well-being. Such blanket bans violate the role of government, and fly in the face of precedents now firmly established by the Supreme Court. The American College of Obstetricians and Gynecologists in January 1997 agreed, and declared that "the intervention of legislative bodies into medical decision making is inappropriate, ill advised, and dangerous."[4]

But there are yet other problems. The federal government has no direct jurisdiction on this matter. Legislation on abortion falls under the authority of the individual states to protect the health and safety of the people. The federal government has no such authority. To bypass this limitation of federal power, attempts to ban D&X are placed in the powers of Congress to regulate interstate commerce. This makes the matter of what physicians do with their patients in their offices a matter of interstate commerce, and opens up a host of dangerous precedents. Thus, it not only intrudes upon the relation of the physician and patient, but also places the decision in a wrongful and threatening regulative location.

Moreover, reactionary political groups have attached themselves to issues like abortion to garner support that enables them to work for policies not related to abortion but which serve special interests. I think here particularly of right-wing candidates who support "free enterprise," the minimalist state, high military spending, low welfare, and reduced taxes. Such an ideology supports the interests of the wealthy and certain right-wing economic and political agenda. The majority of the U.S. people do not endorse such views.

Unfortunately, such tactics—used as wedge issues that tip just enough voters over into a right-wing candidate's camp—have worked in a few elections. Legislation to ban late-term abortions is used exactly for such aims. Meanwhile, people like Sue and Jim are caught in these political machinations while struggling with what may well be the most difficult decision of their lives.

For Congress to deny abortions for health and mental health considerations takes decisions out of the hands of these women and their physicians. It is not merely inappropriate legislative policy, it is political cruelty.

Christian Ethics and Late-Term Abortion

Thus far I have discussed Sue and Jim's situation in terms of federal and state legislation. I have not yet addressed their dilemma from an explicitly Christian ethical standpoint. We must now turn to this.

Can a procedure like D&X be morally permissible after the twenty-fourth week? I must confess that I am dispositionally opposed to such a procedure and to late-term abortions. My reasons are several-fold. First, once the fetus has reached viability (a condition that shifts not only in terms of medical technology but also in individual pregnancy cases, usually between the twenty-fourth and the twenty-sixth week), we are no longer in the same place as when dealing with pregnancy before this pivotal time. Moreover, once a fetus begins to have brain waves (what one ethicist has called "the capacity to experience reality," or what is also called "sentience") in this same period of time, the fetus takes on an emergent characteristic of personhood not present prior to this time in pregnancy.[5] At this point, the potential of personhood comes to a significant actuality. Furthermore, the risk to the health and life of the pregnant woman is much more serious. The question then becomes one of whether there are morally appropriate exceptions to a disposition against late-term abortion.

Here that old question of "When does life begin?" surfaces. The question probably cannot be answered. In a very real sense life does not "begin." There is no break in living cellular structure in the entire fertilization process. Nevertheless, it may be useful to complicate some of the easy answers so often given, especially by some fundamentalist Christians who take absolutist positions against abortion.

First, in Scripture, life is overwhelmingly identified with breath. In Genesis 2, God breathes into Adam "the breath of life." Similar associations of life with breath can be found in Genesis 7:22, 6:17, and 7:15. In Joshua 10:40, 11:10, 14, life is equated with breath. (Compare 1 Kings 17:17, Genesis 35:18, Psalm 104:29-30, and especially Ezekiel 37.) Fundamentalists who argue that Scripture should be believed literally, but who are also antiabortion absolutists, ignore such pervasive testimony.

Two other passages tend to be ignored by biblical literalists. The first of these is Exodus 21:22-25. This passage occurs in one of the oldest collection of laws in the Old Testament, the Book of the Covenant. It reads: "When people who are fighting injure a pregnant woman so that there is a miscarriage, and yet no further harm follows, the one responsible shall be fined what the woman's husband demands, paying as much as the judges determine. If any harm follows, then you shall give life for life, eye for eye, tooth for tooth, hand for hand . . . ." Here the fetus has a monetary value but is not a living person.

The other passage is Numbers 5:11-31. In this passage a woman who is suspected by her husband of being unfaithful is to be taken to the priest. The priest gives her "the water of bitterness," made from holy water and dust from the floor of the tabernacle. If she is innocent, then she is immune to this potion and suffers no consequence. If she is guilty, then this happens: "The LORD make you an execration and an oath among your people, when the LORD makes your uterus drop, your womb discharge; now may this water that brings the curse enter your bowels and make your womb discharge, your uterus drop" (vv. 21-22). This is clearly an instance of the Lord causing a miscarriage because of the woman's unfaithfulness to her husband, and her becoming pregnant by another man. It is the only instance of an "abortion" in Scripture, and it is caused by God.

Usually biblical literalists point to passages like Isaiah 49:1-6, Jeremiah 1:5, and Psalm 139:13-15 to argue that life begins before birth. These references do not suggest that the fetus is a fully human being, nor is this their focus. Rather, they indicate the legitimacy of the call of Isaiah, Jeremiah, and the psalmist to be God's servants. These scriptures certainly say nothing about abortion. They do indicate that God knew Isaiah, Jeremiah, and the psalmist before they were born, and that God called them

"PARTIAL-BIRTH" ABORTION

from the womb. That God knows our forming in the womb, I do not doubt. God also knows every sperm and every ovum before conception. Such divine knowledge does not indicate a beginning of life as biblical literalists suggest.[6]

One final point: The ancient world did not understand that a woman has an egg, as we understand this today. Rather, women were strictly seedbeds for the seed/semen of men. Hence, contemporary discussions of "conception" bring to Scripture a host of ideas and understandings that simply were not a part of the biblical world. To argue that life begins at conception, as in a sperm making contact with a female egg, is not biblical. Moreover, the notion of life beginning when a genetic structure is formed between the woman and the man as a result of fertilization is also not a biblical notion.

Church tradition also leaves us in a confused state. The idea of "ensoulment" was prominent at times in the life of the church. It is interesting that this state occurred sometime after conception, and that baby boys became ensouled before baby girls, reflecting the patriarchy of the times. "Quickening" was also an important event in discussions of when life began, but we now understand that this is more a matter of the sensitivity of the woman than an indication of a new stage in the development of the fetus.

So what do we do with these views? It is not my point to argue for one of these biblical or traditional views about the beginning of life. Rather, my point is that simplistic claims about what the Bible says, especially by biblical literalists, is untenable, and their certitude about life beginning at conception flies in the face of too much of the biblical evidence. The best that can be said in these terms is that the Bible does not help us explicitly with the issue of abortion as such.

With no explicit help from these sources, how can Sue

145

and Jim approach the issue of her pregnancy and depression? From a Christian perspective I would want to approach this matter from the standpoint of what God has done in Christ to establish the kingdom of God, and what it means to be the community of faith called to an intrinsic faithfulness to that reign. As a people of faith, how are we to relate to such deeply conflicted circumstances?

As a community of faith, a Christian response will not simply be some individual choice. While I defend the claim of a woman—alone if need be—finally to make the decision about abortion with her physician, I become increasingly restive with the word *choice*. In a democratic state with individual rights and liberties, this may be consistent with procedural justice, but this is not an adequate Christian stance. Such language makes the "choice" much too singular an act, much too individualistic, and does not place the decision in a larger matrix of communal goods.

The problem with the democratic state is that it cannot have a common good. Virtually by definition it must leave open the question of the good. The form this typically takes in the United States is: "You pursue what you regard as good, and I'll pursue what I regard as good; and as long as we don't interfere with each other, things will be fine." Such a stance may be the best the nation can do, but it is not sufficient for the Christian community. That is, Sue and Jim may be well within their rights as individuals in secular society, but what about their commitment as Christians? My point here is not to challenge *Roe v. Wade*, because I do not know how our form of government can pursue a policy any different and still be consistent with the Constitution and American civil liberties and rights. The Christian community, however, has as its good the reign of God. Our mission is to live faithfully now in lives and practices that are intrinsic to that realm. By *intrinsic* I mean that these are practices that instantiate that reign—to be sure, in broken ways—in the here and now. That means that if the reign of God is a welcoming place, a place of hospitality, then we are to be a welcoming community, a community of hospitality. We must especially welcome children. It is a basic virtue of Christian community.

That ethical stance makes character and virtue central. This means we do not believe that ethics consists simply of making good or right choices only on the basis of the situational circumstances at hand. Christian ethics is not a situational ethic. Rather, Christian ethics has to do with certain dispositions one brings to situations that shape the kinds of decisions one will make or not make. Such a position can make exceptions, but the exception is not the rule. Such an ethics is not based on exceptional cases. In this sense, virtue becomes very important in the formation of our character. By practicing virtues we shape and form our dispositions. Hence, a Christian ethic would not simply argue that because one has a right to a certain choice it is therefore ethical. One can have a right in terms of United States legal procedure that is not ethical for a Christian, in that it is a violation of the goods and virtues of the reign of God. One of these virtues is hospitality. We have responsibility before God to welcome the stranger, the marginal, the person outside the gate. We certainly have a responsibility to welcome children. As Christians, our disposition is to be hospitable to the little ones.[7]

At the same time, a disposition is not an absolute. While we do not build a Christian ethic on exceptional cases, exceptional cases do exist. And, indeed, while virtues are the central practices of the Christian faith, what is to be done when a person is not capable of performing the virtue? Here I think of the virtue of hospitality. If, indeed, Sue's depression will increase steadily with the pregnancy, as her doctor believes in his best medical judgment, she will not be able to perform the role of a hospitable host.

I am making a delicate point here: There is nothing else in all of creation like pregnancy and birth. Nothing else is comparable to it. For one thing, no one else can do it for Sue. If she increasingly cannot be hospitable to the fetus, what then becomes of a virtue of hospitality imposed on one unable to fulfill it. For the church to insist that she continue a practice for which she is incapable is for the church to engage in a practice also contrary to the reign of God—the expectation of responsibility for one unable to be accountable.

Circumstances like Sue and Jim's are tragic in a late-term abortion. With Sue's health condition and her decision to pursue a D&X, a healthy fetus will be killed. At twenty-four weeks the fetus may already have brain waves and the lung capacity to live outside the womb. Such decisions ought never to be simple policy for Christians. That is, our ethics are based on the development of character and the practice of virtues that bring to situations special resources and capacities to cope and find alternative ways to choose life, and is not based on policy that is formed primarily by exceptional cases that can blur practices that are intrinsic to the life of faith. Again, ethics is not built on exceptional cases.

In cases like Sue and Jim's, the disposition to welcome must not become an oppressive claim on those unable to be hosts. To insist that a woman be hospitable when she herself needs shelter is hardly a Kingdom virtue. To insist that she be hospitable when she needs a hospital is cruelty.[8]

I realize, of course, that a decision like Sue's does value the woman more than the fetus. Yet, as tragic as a choice of any kind like this is, it is a valuation that is quite clearly held by the overwhelming majority of people of faith, namely Christians and Jews. When one allows late-term abortion for the sake of the woman's life, such an evaluation is clearly made.

It is not my intention to provide some kind of open-door policy for late-term abortions. The use of D&X in a late-term abortion with a physically and mentally healthy woman and a healthy fetus is wrong.

Conclusion

I contend that it is morally permissible for Sue to proceed with the D&X procedure early in the third trimester of her pregnancy. In the physician's opinion, Sue's condition is of such severity as to make her unable to carry a late-term pregnancy to completion and sustain her mental health. In a Christian ethics that takes with the utmost seriousness the reign of God and the virtue of hospitality to children, there must yet be the place for the exceptional case, not in an ethics based on exceptions, but in one that admits them to moral deliberation in a world where things are not right. Moreover, these are precisely the kinds of circumstances that legislatures cannot address by abstract bans of law. These are areas where legislatures do not have competence, and where in our own time these matters are so often decided by political machinations that have little or no concern for the circumstances of the pregnant woman or her fetus. Government should cease and desist.

NOTES

1. I am indebted here to John M. Swomley, Jr., "The 'Partial-Birth' Debate in 1998," *The Humanist* (March/April 1998): 7.
2. H.R. 1833, 104th Congress.
3. *Roe v. Wade,* 410 U.S. 113 (1973). See also *Doe v. Bolton,* 410 U.S. 179, 192 (1973); and *Planned Parenthood of Southeastern Pennsylvania v. Casey,* 502 U.S. 1056 (1993).

4. American College of Obstetrics and Gynecology. Statement on intact dilation and extraction, 12 January 1997. In this connection, George J. Annas raises three questions that are on target in terms of this legislative debate: (1) What is the appropriate role of government in regulating health care? (2) Should decisions about specific medical procedures be made by physicians or Congress? (3) The issue of who (the medical profession or the state health plans, for that matter) has the authority to determine what is and what is not a legitimate medical procedure has implications for everything done by physicians, not just for abortions. See George J. Annas, "Partial-Birth Abortion, Congress, and the Constitution," *New England Journal of Medicine,* 339/4 (23 July 1998): 281.

5. J. Philip Wogaman, *Abortion: Shall We Return to Absolution? The Supreme Court in Moral Perspective* (Washington, D.C.: The Religious Coalition for Abortion Rights, 1974).

6. See, for example, Charles Baughman, "Yahveh Called Me from the Womb," *Christian Social Action* (July/August 1996): 26-29, esp. 29.

7. The most compelling case against my own position on abortion is the position of Stanley Hauerwas. See the article by him and Joel Shuman in this volume.

8. I have focused here on the case of Sue and Jim, but there is a much larger group of disadvantaged women and children under sixteen years of age who face late-term abortions. See David A. Grimes, "The Continuing Need for Late Abortions," *Journal of the American Medical Association,* 280/8 (8 August 1998): 6.

CAN "PARTIAL-BIRTH" ABORTION BE A LEGITIMATE MORAL CHOICE?

A Response by Joan Burgess Winfrey

I am an evangelical, pro-life feminist. These are not mutually exclusive categories. As an evangelical, I believe that the sanctity of life and quality of life rests on the reality of a loving, creator God and that all persons are created in the image of God. Being pro-life, I affirm that all persons have intrinsic, eternal value, and Christians are called to have a reverence for life. As a feminist, I am committed to a wide array of concerns for the well-being and spiritual wholeness of all women. Thus, I concur with the distress of pro-choice Jewish author Naomi Wolf, who has courageously called pro-choice feminism to a place of truth and accountability.[1]

James T. Burtchaell, a former professor at Notre Dame, is another voice that systematically challenges arguments typically advanced in the pro-choice debate. Twenty years ago he spoke of "magic moment assertions" sponsored by those unwilling to acknowledge that "the unborn to be eliminated is an infant human being."[2] Terms such as *quickening, viability, potential person,* and *fetal material* have been used to locate the moment of humanification during prenatal or postnatal development. As he said succinctly, "You can't have it both ways; medical scientists claim they are creating human life in a test tube. You can't call it something else in the womb."[3]

Scripturally, we do not find a distinction made between the child in the womb and the full-grown adult. In Psalm

139:13-14, David says, "For you created my inmost being; you knit me together in my mother's womb. I praise you because I am fearfully and wonderfully made" (NIV). We could, in like manner find references to Samuel the Prophet (1 Samuel 1:17-19) and John the Baptist (Luke 1:13-17) while they were forming in the bodies of Hannah and Elizabeth respectively. The great themes of Scripture return us always to reverence for life, and humble praise to the God who is the creator of life and the lover of our souls. The implications arising from this truth are instructive as to how we must then live in relationship to one another.

Arguments Against Partial-Birth Abortion

The tragic truth that emerges out of even a superficial understanding of the issues surrounding partial-birth abortion is that we are not a culture willing or able to provide care or caring toward those who are regarded as high maintenance. These include the unwanted child, especially if the child is imperfect, or anyone else who detracts from our pursuit of "a quality life."

Any argument against the procedure that is known as "partial-birth" abortion must hold in juxtaposition a constellation of legal, moral, and scientific considerations. The legal reasoning used to affirm abortion is couched in two major arguments: the right to privacy, and the primacy of individual choice. These must be examined in light of their tragic cultural consequences—the needless death of thousands of unborn children, and a curious array of aberrant court decisions such as "wrongful birth" and "wrongful life" that have their basis in *Roe v. Wade*.

The moral/theological debate engendered by the practice of partial-birth abortion must, of necessity, be placed in the larger context of the abortion issue in general. Significantly, however, partial-birth abortion has pressed into sharp relief the incoherence of pro-choice discussions about personhood and humanness and their ontological meanings. The scientific body of knowledge accumulated over several decades had brought an infusion of new information that can be called "truth serum." Though the most common reasons given for this type of late-term abortion are the endangered life of the mother, or the abnormality or deformity of the fetus, advances in embryology, perinatology, and maternal care have shifted the ground beneath the rationalizations and euphemisms that have undergirded abortion on demand.

Medical Necessity: Euphemism or Equivocation?

The technique that is commonly referred to as "partial-birth" abortion is known in medical terms as intact dilation and extraction. It is a surgical procedure, described earlier in this chapter, used to induce abortion during the second and third trimesters of pregnancy, and has been utilized in some cases up to full term. Epner, Jones, and Seckinger, in the *Journal of the American Medical Association,* describe the technique as "a specific procedure comprising the following elements: deliberate dilation of the cervix, usually over a sequence of days; instrumental or manual conversion of the fetus to a footling breech; breech extraction of the body except the head; and partial evacuation of the intracranial contents of the living fetus to effect vaginal delivery of a dead, but otherwise intact, fetus."[4]

The tragic reality is this. There is no time when a viable, preterm fetus must be killed in order to save the mother's life. Viability is a legal-medical concept and is ascertained by the capacity of the fetus to survive indefinitely outside of the uterus, with or without medical assistance. A mother with a serious medical need is treated first and foremost. This can mean the preterm delivery of her infant—it will remain her decision. No obstetrician would choose to place a mother's life in extreme jeopardy to sustain a fetus without the mother's consent.

Additionally, there is little medical argument against the induced delivery of a dead, severely deformed, or medically untreatable fetus that would be nonviable. These cases are very rare and are not the issue. Indeed, reference to such cases distorts the principle on which partial-birth abortion is opposed. The sole issue is the disposition of the preterm, viable fetus. No medical literature supports the need to intentionally kill a viable fetus in order to save the mother's life. This unborn child is literally three centimeters away from full protection of the law.[5]

A final medical component to the argument against the use of partial-birth abortion is recent advances in perinatology (prenatal and postnatal care of fetuses and infants). These advances continue to enhance the survivability of premature babies. Currently, viability may range from twenty-two to twenty-seven weeks or 500 grams of weight.

Prior to the child's birth, ultrasound allows for Doppler scanning; the heart's functioning and blood circulation can be determined. If there is a concern about blood flow, the unborn child can be given blood or receive a blood transfusion. Peri-umbilical blood sampling (PUBS) is a new diagnostic method for monitoring fetal health. Intrauterine surgeries may alleviate or correct abnormalities.[6]

Physicians have been compelled to provide to the public accurate information about partial-birth abortion. The Physicians' Ad Hoc Coalition for Truth, an organization of more than three hundred members, made the following statement:

> We are the physicians who on a daily basis treat pregnant women and their babies. And we can no longer remain silent while abortion activists, the media, and even the Pres-

ident of the United States continue to repeat false medical claims about partial-birth abortion. The appalling lack of medical credibility on the side of those defending this procedure has forced us—for the first time in our professional careers—to leave the sidelines in order to provide some sorely needed facts in a debate that has been dominated by anecdote, emotion, and media stunts. Contrary to what abortion activists would have us to believe, partial-birth abortion is never medically indicated to protect a woman's health or her fertility. In fact, the opposite is true. The procedure can pose a significant and immediate threat to both the pregnant woman's health and her fertility.[7]

Abortion and Slavery

Perhaps the doctors who have stepped forward to inform the public about partial-birth abortion are the Harriet Beecher Stowes of the present generation. Several authors have drawn parallels between the deeper moral issues of slavery and those of abortion. Both subjects distill quickly to discussions of value and reverence for life. Several authors, including Paul Johnson—historian and social critic, have depicted frightening parallels between historical rationales for slavery, and current rationales for abortion.

> Slavery was tolerable only when it was shrouded in ignorance, euphemism, and deception. The more you knew about its realities, the more its ugly facts were uncovered, the higher the gorge rose . . . Harriet Beecher Stowe in *Uncle Tom's Cabin* brought the horrible essence of slavery home to millions of readers in an emotional form they found irresistible.[8]

Mackubin T. Owens, professor at the Naval War College, finds an eerie parallel between the words of Abraham

155

Lincoln, spoken about Stephen Douglas during their first joint debate, and the words of pro-choice feminist Naomi Wolf. Lincoln says of Douglas:

> When he invites any people willing to have slavery to establish it, he is blowing out the moral lights around us. When he says he "cares not whether slavery is voted up or voted down"—that it is a sacred right of self-government —he is, in my judgment, penetrating the human soul and eradicating the light of reason and the love of liberty in this American people.[9]

Naomi Wolf wrote:

> We [of the pro-choice movement] stand in jeopardy of losing what can only be called our souls. Clinging to a rhetoric about abortion in which there is no life and no death, we entangle ourselves in a series of self-delusions, fibs, and evasions. And we risk becoming precisely what our critics charge us with being: callous, selfish, and casually destructive men and women who share a cheapened view of life.[10]

Owens likens the Supreme Court decision of *Dred Scott* in 1857, which helped shape public opinion that slavery was a "sacred right" not to be interfered with by the government, with *Roe v. Wade*, which gives legal sanction to abortion as an absolute right. The *Dred Scott* decision determined that African Americans were not persons, just as *Roe v. Wade* and the subsequent decisions based upon its ruling denied the status of personhood to an unborn child.

Prevalence of Partial-Birth Abortion

The horrors of partial-birth abortion are magnified by the fact that it is an entirely unnecessary procedure. The horror is greater when we read the prevalence reports. There is considerable variation among the reports, making prevalence difficult to establish. We must give earnest heed, however, to the statements of physicians who perform this procedure. The numbers, even if we tally only a handful of these self-reports, far exceed the total yearly numbers in the U.S. reported by the Alan Guttmacher Institute, the research arm of Planned Parenthood.[11] The Institute has reported numbers as low as five hundred to six hundred per year. The Centers for Disease Control, however, reported yearly numbers of late-term abortions as high as seventeen thousand.[12] A former official at Mt. Sinai Hospital told of a clinic in New Jersey that said of the three thousand abortions it did last year, fifteen hundred were late-term.[13]

Political Stratagem: The Tangled Web We Weave

In 1998, the United States Senate failed to overturn, for the second time, President Clinton's veto of an act banning partial-birth abortion. The first veto was in April 1996. Ostensibly, the president vetoed the bills in both cases because they would prohibit partial-birth abortions where severe injury, massive health damage, or permanent disability would occur to the woman because of the pregnancy. The president's stated reasons for banning the bills obscure a broader political blueprint than the seemingly benign, pro-woman stance suggested in his comments.

A Harvard law professor, Mary Ann Glendon, in her 1996 testimony, given before a congressional committee, took issue with President Clinton's stance, particularly his claim that the act was unconstitutional.[14] She believes his position misreads *Roe v. Wade* and subsequent abortion decisions. However, his position reflects an all too accurate understanding of the core holding of *Roe:* that abortion is constitutionally protected in the United States through the ninth month of pregnancy for almost any reason the mother may assert.

It was not the Constitution that forced the veto pen of the president, as neither *Roe* nor later abortion decisions say anything about the right to kill a child during the course of delivery, and the Supreme Court has never directly addressed a law like the Partial-Birth Abortion Ban Act. Such a question could not arise in most other legal systems; late-term abortions are either forbidden or carefully regulated almost everywhere. It is Glendon's conclusion that the United States has reaped from *Roe* a coarsening not only of our laws, but also of our hearts. Polls indicate that a majority of Americans are uneasy about late-term abortions, yet a majority say they support *Roe v. Wade.* "Since *Roe* constitutionally protects, in most circumstances, those late-term abortions about which the public is so uneasy, somehow the truth about *Roe* is not getting out."[15]

Roe, with its basis in the fundamental right to privacy, has resulted in a whole new exploration of rights that further serve to erode respect for life. For example, "wrongful life" is a legal action in which a child can sue a doctor for failure to find a defect that might have spurred the mother to abort the child. "Wrongful birth" provides damages to the mother for failure of her doctor to obtain informed consent to continue with the pregnancy despite the risks. The record must show the mother was informed of the risks. Furthermore, Thomas Goodwin has pointed out the lack of clear legal guidelines that would assist the doctor in determining which risks warrant consent.[16]

Obviously, these wrongful-life suits discriminate against people with disabilities. In the early 1980s, I served as a political action network coordinator in Colorado on behalf of the educational rights of children with disabilities. Patricia Schroeder, former representative of Colorado, has consistently been a stalwart supporter of legislation that protected those rights; therefore, I was shocked and deeply disappointed to read her testimonies given on the House floor in April 1996 garnering support for partial-birth abortion. Highly offended at the prospect of the display of charts depicting the procedure, Schroeder threatened retaliation by bringing in pictures of severely handicapped children.[17]

Restoring Our Souls

Condoning partial-birth abortions, in my judgment, is immoral and unchristian. The reflections of Jean Rostand are reminiscent of the teachings of Jesus and need to be underscored both in church and society. Rostand declares:

> I have the weakness to believe that it is an honor for a society to desire the expensive luxury of sustaining life for its useless, incompetent, and incurably ill members. I would almost measure a society's degree of civilization by the amount of effort and vigilance it imposes on itself out of pure respect of life. It is noble to struggle unrelentingly to save someone's life, as if he were dear to us, when objectively he has no value and is not even loved by anyone.[18]

Ultimately, I believe that both an individual and a culture are to be evaluated and judged by the treatment "the least of these" are accorded in a society. The prophet Micah brings the six hundred thirteen points of Old Testament law down to only three: "To act justly and to love mercy and to walk humbly with your God" (Micah 6:8 NIV).

To whom shall we look as an example of Micah's law fulfilled? Let me suggest two ideal models serve our purpose. One is Mother Teresa, who retrieved the outcast, the diseased, the despised, and the dying from the squalid gutters of Calcutta, and found holy joy in the doing of it. Another is Henri Nouwen, who left the academic life at Princeton to love and care for the mentally retarded residents of the L'Arche ministry, and found soul transformation in the doing of it. Finally, let us look to the example of the Wounded Healer, Jesus Christ, who loved us and gave himself for us, that we might have life.

We must choose life, and in so doing, heal our souls and the soul of the nation. Prohibiting partial-birth abortions would be a significant moral step in the right direction.

NOTES

1. Naomi Wolf, "Our Bodies, Our Souls," in *New Republic*, 16 October 1995. Reprinted in *Human Life Review* (Winter 1997): 45-59.
2. James T. Burtchaell, *Rachel Weeping: The Case Against Abortion* (New York: Harper & Row, 1982), p. 87.
3. Ibid., p. 82.
4. Janet E. Epner, Ph.D., Harry S. Jones, M.D., and Daniel L. Seckinger, M.D., "Special Communication: Late-Term Abortion," in *Journal of the American Medical Association*, vol. 280, no. 8 (26 August 1998): 729.
5. Timothy Durkee, M.D., Ph.D., "Partial-Birth Abortion," unpublished paper, 1998.
6. Medical information about partial-birth abortion was obtained through telephone interviews with Timothy Durkee, M.D., Ph.D., and James Miller, M.D., in December 1998 and January 1999. Both physicians are members of the Department of Obstetrics and Gynecology at the University of Illinois College of Medicine at Rockford, and physicians in private practice. Dr. Miller chairs the department.
7. *Wall Street Journal*, 19 September 1996, editorial page.
8. Paul Johnson, "It Is Not True That There Are No Other Good Causes—Ending Abortion Is One," *The Human Life Review* (Fall 1996): appendix F.
9. Mackubin Thomas Owens, "Slavery and Abortion: Let Us Readopt the Declaration," *The Human Life Review* (Fall 1996): 65-70.
10. Ibid., p. 68.
11. National Right to Life Committee, "Why Are Partial-Birth Abortions Performed?" Web site *www.nrlc.org*, 21 October 1998; and Abortion Law Homepage; "'Partial-Birth' Abortion Laws," Internet site *http://members.aol.com*, 21 September 1998.

12. Ibid.

13. Mike Royke, "Doctors See Lies Behind Reasons for Late-Term Abortion," issued 28 February 1997 and reprinted in *The Human Life Review* (Spring 1997): 87-88.

14. Testimony before the Subcommittee on the Constitution of the Judiciary Committee of the United States House of Representatives, 22 April 1996, pp. 55-64.

15. Ibid.

16. Thomas Murphy Goodwin, "Medicalizing Abortion Decision," *First Things* (March 1996): 33-36. Goodwin is assistant professor of Obstetrics and Gynecology at the University of Southern California, and director of Maternal Fetal Medicine at the Good Samaritan Hospital in Los Angeles.

17. The Congressional Record, 1 November 1995.

18. Jean Rostand, "Humanly Possible: A Biologist's Notes on the Future of Mankind," trans. Lowell Blair in *Saturday Review Press* (1973), as quoted by Burtchaell in *Rachel Weeping: The Case Against Abortion.*

QUESTIONS

1. Based on what you know from science, along with your faith convictions, how do you answer the question, When does life begin?
2. Many authors writing in this section struggle with the ethics of "seldom" versus "never." Do you believe that God calls us to obey absolute rules forbidding abortion, or do you believe that an ethic of love requires us to allow for exceptions?
3. If one believes exceptions can be made to legitimate certain abortions, by what criteria should these exceptions be made? For example, are incest and rape different from a late-term or partial-birth abortion to save the life of the mother? If so, on what moral grounds?
4. If you were faced with valuing a potential infant's life versus the total well-being of the mother, what criteria do you think should be considered? Criteria might include not only ethical principles but also human factors like a potential mother's age, family support, socioeconomic status, and so forth.
5. Have you ever had a daughter, friend, or colleague whose life circumstances led her to consider an abortion? How did you feel about her decision?
6. In what ways can faith communities offer God's love and hospitality to mothers who lack family support and financial resources in order to rear children who were not planned?
7. If a potential infant has serious physical or mental "defects," is abortion morally legitimate?

PART THREE

CLONING:
A FORBIDDEN FRUIT?

CHAPTER EIGHT

THE MEANING OF LIFE AND CLONES

Lee M. Silver

When does a human being come into existence? Among all the questions asked by ethicists and theologians, this one is probably the most critical to the way in which ethical decisions are made on a daily basis. Ethical people of all religious and political persuasions agree that human beings should be treated with dignity and respect. We all agree that slavery, abuse, and the murder of human beings are intolerable actions. In contrast, we must all kill other living things to sustain our lives. Thoughtful people may worry about the infliction of pain on higher animals, but if they are not vegetarian, they accept the killing of mammals for food and usually for medical research as well. (Even strict vegetarians crush living cells to death as they eat their garden salads.)

When Life Begins

Many people believe that science can play no role in determining when human life begins, and that this question should be left to the realm of theology. But we now know this assumption is false. Just as twentieth-century science has given us great insight into when and how the universe began (although not why), it has given us great insight into when and how human beings come into existence (although, once again, not why).

Before we can understand what science tells us about the beginning of human life, it is necessary to understand what we mean by the term "human life" itself. Much confusion has been sowed by the unfortunate use of this term in two very different ways.[1] This single term is used to describe conscious individuals as well as individual human cells that scientists can grow indefinitely in the laboratory. The distinction between these two usages is best exemplified by considering what happens right after someone is shot to death with a bullet to the heart. The person is clearly dead even though 90 percent of the cells in the body are still alive. Indeed, some of the dead person's organs can continue to function if they are transplanted into the bodies of other persons!

Aristotle clearly understood the different meanings of life when he proposed the division of the soul into three components: vegetative (or nutritive), animal, and human.[2] With modern science, we can interpret Aristotle's vegetative soul as being equivalent to cellular life, his animal soul as being equivalent to a functional nervous system (in any animal), and his human soul as being equivalent to human consciousness.

Every time you blow your nose, scratch your skin, or take a shower, you kill living cells, but no sane person mourns their death. Thus, it would seem that human life at the cellular level (Aristotle's vegetative soul) is simply not deserving of our respect. However, until 1997, there was near-universal belief that the one-cell human embryo was different in some fundamental way from other cells in the body because it alone had the potential to form a new human life. Based on this perceived difference, many bioethicists were willing to grant the one-cell human embryo special respect and protection from experimentation.

On February 27 of that year, Dolly, the first animal cloned from an adult cell was announced to the world.

But what was missed by many people in the media fanfare was the revolutionary implication that this one animal had for the status of human embryos. In one fell swoop, Dolly's birth shattered the illusion of a line separating human cells with the potential to form a new life from those without such potential.

What Dolly tells scientists is that there is no metaphysical difference between any living cell with a complete set of human genes. They all have the potential to become reprogrammed to start anew the development of a conscious human being. *Potential* is the key word here. It does not mean that we actually want to do it, it does not mean that we have the technical capability of doing it today, and it does not mean that it will ever be efficient with some cells. But it makes no sense to suggest that different degrees of potentiality (determined simply by the currently available technology) should cause us to view an embryo cell as being ethically different from a cell scratched off your skin.

It is important to understand exactly what makes an embryo cell behave differently from a skin cell. Both have the same DNA with the same genetic code. But at the outset, they have different proteins loosely attached to different regions of that DNA. The type and location of proteins on the DNA determines the portion of the genetic program that is being run, which, in turn, determines the behavior and "potential" of the cell. At the moment, with our primitive knowledge, we can only blindly restart the genetic program of an adult cell by fusing it with an unfertilized egg. But once we understand exactly what proteins are involved, it may become possible to simply add those proteins directly to a skin cell to convert it into an embryo.

So what reasons could we have for treating a one-cell human embryo differently from a skin cell? There are only two. Either the positioning of protein molecules on

DNA is determinative of whether a human cell is deserving of our respect, or we must believe that once a cell becomes an embryo, it is imbued with a special spirit or higher-level soul that does not exist in other cells.

But there is a problem with the "soul in a one-cell embryo" hypothesis that is best illustrated with the following thought experiment: Let us imagine that in vitro fertilization has been used to produce a single embryo for a couple who have been trying for a very long time to have children. The couple realize that it might not be possible to have another embryo produced, and they decide they want to turn their one embryo into two babies. To accommodate their wishes, a fertility doctor waits for the embryo to develop to the two-cell stage and then pulls the cells apart so that there are now two one-cell embryos with the potential to develop into identical twins. (Such a process occurs naturally in people and is easy to accomplish in the lab as well.) If you believe that every one-cell embryo is imbued with a soul, then two souls exist in these two embryos.

Quickly, however, the couple changes their mind. They decide that it is too difficult to raise two children at the same time, and they really only want to have one baby. So, the fertility doctor pushes the two embryos back together to produce the single embryo that the couple started with, which could develop into a single normal child.

What has been lost in this process? All of the cells started with are still alive, so no one has killed anything. The only thing that is possibly lost is a human soul, but where did the second soul come from when the cells were pulled apart, and where did it go when they were put back together?

Milestones on the Pathway to Life

If the one-cell human embryo is no different metaphysically from a cell you scratch off your skin, when during embryogenesis does a significant difference arise? Unfortunately, there is no simple answer to this question. One problem is that development is slow and continuous. There are no isolated moments along the way where a person can point at an embryo or fetus and say that it is substantially different from the way it was a few minutes, or even hours, earlier. Nevertheless, during the nine-month period of gestation, the embryo and fetus pass through a series of major developmental stages during which important milestones on the pathway to human life are reached. Through an appreciation for the significance of these milestones, it becomes possible for each of us to make an informed decision on the question of the emergence of human life.

The first important milestone occurs between ten and fourteen days after conception. At this time, the free-floating embryo latches onto the uterine wall and implants itself. The embryo begins a period of rapid growth and the individual cells in the embryo begin to distinguish themselves from each other so that twinning is no longer possible. The very first cells that will eventually develop into the spinal cord also make their appearance.

During the fourth week, one can see the beginnings of the gut, liver, and heart. At the end of the fourth week, the heart is beating and primitive blood cells are moving along embryonic veins and arteries. It is also at this stage that the very earliest development of the brain begins. Still, the embryo is less than a quarter of an inch long.

Between six and eight weeks after fertilization, the embryo turns into—what appears to be—a miniature human being with arms, legs, hands, feet, fingers, toes, eyes, ears, and nose. It is these external humanlike features that cause a shift in terminology from embryo to fetus. By twelve weeks, the inside of the fetus has also become rather humanlike, with the appearance of all the major organs. The first trimester of pregnancy is now completed.

Although looks alone can have a powerful effect on how we view something, it is important to understand what is, and what is not, present at this early stage of fetal development. While major organs can be recognized, they have not yet begun to function. Although the cerebral cortex—the eventual seat of human awareness and emotions—has begun to grow, the cells within it are not capable of functioning as nerve cells. They are simply precursors to nerve cells without the ability to send or receive any neurological signals. Further steps of differentiation must occur before they even look like nerves or develop the ability to make synaptic contacts with each other. And in the absence of communication among nerve cells, there cannot be any consciousness. This means that if a fetus is aborted at this stage, it cannot feel any pain.

Two independent milestones occur between the twenty-fourth and twenty-sixth weeks after conception. The first is viability. It is during this period that the fetus develops the ability to survive outside the womb. Survival becomes possible as the fetal lungs begin to function for the first time. The second critical milestone is the wiring up of the cerebral cortex, and with this functionality comes the first potential for human consciousness. When consciousness itself actually arises is impossible to know. While people have different definitions of consciousness, they all refer to some concept of a mental state that defines each of us as individual persons. No matter what the definition is, it is quite separate from the simple viability of a human body. In theory, it is possible for a baby to be born with just a brain stem (controlling heart and lung functions) and no higher brain. This anacephalic baby would be less conscious than a fish (probably even a worm) and it would not even feel pain, and yet it would be viable (if it were fed through tubes).

The Possibility of Human Cloning

At this point, it is worthwhile to end with a discussion concerning the possibility of human cloning. Much of the public misunderstanding of what scientists can actually accomplish with cloning is based on the failure of most people to distinguish cellular human life from conscious human life. The replication of conscious human life is now, and always will be, impossible. The only thing that scientists will ever be able to clone in any organism is cellular life. Success has already been achieved with three different mammalian species—cows, sheep, and mice—and there is every reason to believe that human embryos could be cloned as well.

Many people are frightened by the prospect of human cloning. But more often than not, their fears derive from aspects of the popular conceptualization of cloning that have no basis in reality. There is the worry that evil governments or groups will clone large numbers of warriors (or factory workers, or geniuses) who are beholden to their maker; that cloning will exacerbate the world population explosion; that cloning will interfere with evolution; that clones will be bred for body parts; or that egomaniacs will clone themselves to achieve immortality.

Even people educated enough to understand the real biological process of cloning can have an exaggerated belief in how similar a child conceived through such a process will be to his or her progenitor. Religious scholar Leon Kass expresses the views of others when he writes that "cloning creates serious issues of identity and individuality. . . . The cloned individual will be saddled with a genotype that has already lived. He will not be fully a surprise to the world."[3]

All of these fears are groundless, because the real biological process accomplishes so much less than people imagine. Children conceived by cloning will be indistinguishable from children conceived naturally (in the absence of a DNA test that compares the child to the progenitor). Like all other children, they will be born as infants from women after nine months of gestation. Like all other children (including identical twins), each one will be a unique human being with a unique identity and an unpredictable future. And it would be no less an act of murder to remove the heart of such a child for transplantation than it would be to remove any other child's heart (which is why no legitimate medical clinic would consider such a thing).[4]

Whereas genes play an important role in guiding the development of our bodies, they do not determine who we become. It will be no more possible to predict how a cloned child will turn out than to predict how any other child will turn out. It is for this very basic reason, if none other, that real biological cloning will be of no use to governments or egomaniacs. If governments want people with certain abilities or skills, it would be quicker and more efficient for them to institute an appropriate system of universal education and then identify those citizens who demonstrate the desired characteristics. Egomaniacs, by definition, care only about themselves and no one else; they will quickly lose interest in cloning when they understand that it will not allow them to achieve immortality (and they could end up with a child who will not even listen to them).

If reproductive cloning accomplishes so little, why would anyone possibly want to do it? The answer lies within the single thing that cloning can accomplish—it can provide a person with a biologically related child. Anyone who expects anything more from reproductive cloning than an unpredictable son or daughter to love will be sorely disappointed.

NOTES

1. For a detailed discussion on the two different scientific meanings of the term "human life," see chapter 1 of Lee M. Silver, *Remaking Eden: How Genetic Engineering and Cloning Will Transform the American Family* (New York: Avon Books, 1998).

2. Aristotle, *On the Soul* (New York: Oxford Press, 1941), p. 560.

3. L. R. Kass and J. Q. Wilson, *The Ethics of Human Cloning* (Washington, D.C.: American Enterprise Institute Press, 1998).

4. Editors' Note: Recent reports in newspapers and popular magazines have left many laypeople with the impression that newborn clones show signs of aging because their cells are the age of their parent's cells. Reputable scientists, however, are much less sure about the validity of this conclusion made from preliminary data. For example, a scientist from the National Institute on Aging called the results "a little messy."

CHAPTER NINE

SHOULD HUMAN CLONING BE PERMITTED?

Overview

M olecular biologist Lee M. Silver asserts that science does play a role in determining when life begins. Using Aristotle's model, Silver says that a human soul is equivalent to human consciousness. Everyone kills living cells of one type or another. The cloning of Dolly the sheep told scientists that there is "no metaphysical difference between any living cell with a complete set of human genes." The cells could be reprogrammed to develop a conscious human being. During gestation the embryo and fetus pass through a series of major developmental stages leading to human life. Silver notes the milestones, differentiating between the points of viability and consciousness.

Public misunderstanding about cloning stems from failure "to distinguish cellular human life from conscious human life." Scientists can clone only cellular, not conscious, life. Cloned children will not be different from children conceived naturally—they will be born after nine months of gestation. Silver says "each one will be a unique human being with a unique identity and an unpredictable future." The value of cloning will be to create biologically related children.

But should human cloning be permitted? Is it ethical? Authors Rabbi Gerald L. Zelizer and practical theologian Abigail Rian Evans offer dramatically contrasting views. On theological and ethical grounds, Zelizer welcomes cloning, and Evans opposes it.

Zelizer rejects the arguments of those wanting to ban the cloning process, fearing religious leaders and laity "have rushed too quickly to fence off this next technological frontier." Without hesitation, he endorses "cloning humans as a strategy to overcome infertility." Reviewing the moral issues posed by cloning, he argues that they justify regulating cloning but not banning. Cloning itself is morally neutral; if used "to work and preserve the world, it is morally acceptable." Citing biblical and pastoral evidence regarding infertility, Zelizer contends that cloning is a "natural solution that responds to the grief of God." He rejects arguments that (1) humans are "playing God," (2) cloning "ruptures the divinely intended tie between love and the conjugal act," and (3) human identity and diversity will be destroyed. Religious folk should embrace cloning that alleviates human suffering. It "assists, rather than undermines, the Almighty."

Evans, on the other hand, opposes cloning, citing nine different reasons. Among them are concerns that cloning treats people as means rather than ends; it undermines the structure of the family; it may be used for morally wrong motives; it separates the creature from the Creator; and it causes a loss of genetic diversity. Deploring the hysterics of much cloning opposition, she notes that even the scientific community is cautious about endorsing it. Evans recognizes both the potential good and evil that might result in the use of cloning. Every person is unique regardless of the method of birthing; a clone is simply a "noncontemporaneous twin." However, Evans fears people will begin to ask, Who needs God when we have the geneticist? and begin to see a cloned child as a "manufactured product instead of a gift from God." Weighing all the factors, she opposes proceeding with cloning "now or in the future."

SHOULD HUMAN CLONING BE PERMITTED?

A Response by Gerald L. Zelizer

The dispute over human cloning was revved up another notch with the successful cloning of mice in 1998 by Japanese scientists in a Hawaiian laboratory. Lee Silver, professor of molecular biology, ecology, and evolutionary biology at Princeton University, predicted that this giant step will lead to "in vitro fertilization clinics adding human cloning to their repertoires within five to ten years." Earlier that same year, Richard Seed, a physicist in Chicago whose expertise is in fertility research, announced that he intends to assemble a team of experts with the purpose of cloning a human being. All this followed the vanguard cloning of a mammal, Dolly the Sheep, in Scotland's Rostin Institute in 1996.

The Seesaw Battle Between Science and Religion

These incremental steps toward the cloning of humans constitute individual struggles in the seesaw battle between science and religion. Previous attempts to defeat bills in the Congress that would have banned cloning were encouraged by the letter of twenty-seven Nobel Prize winners who objected that the proposed legislation would impede scientific research. An earlier victory belonged to the religious side, which succeeded in persuading the president to prohibit the use of federal funding for human cloning investigation. Hovering in between is a voluntary five-year moratorium on the cloning of human beings, established by President Clinton and adopted by the American Society for Reproductive Medicine.

Many religious voices echo the concern of R. Albert Mohler, Jr., that cloning represents the attempt of the creature to be the Creator. We should be extremely reluctant to tamper in any way with the reproductive process our creator has put in place. I fear this will lead inevitably to attempts toward the development of a master race and custom species.[1] Thomas Murray, a member of the President's Bioethics Advisory Committee, has expressed his uneasiness about interfering with advances in science. But he also confesses to even more uneasiness about tampering with a moral and social sense of what it means to be a human being. Prominent Christian periodicals such as *The Christian Century*[2] and *Christianity Today*[3] weighed in with similar objections in their editorials. And this was one instance where those in the pew agreed with those on the pulpit. In a *Time* magazine survey that asked, "Is it against God's will to clone humans?" 74 percent said it was, and 19 percent said it was not.

I fear that both religious leaders and laypeople have rushed too quickly to fence off this next technological frontier.

At an earlier crossroads, that of birth surrogacy, a physician and his wife in my community were one of the first couples in the United States to venture forth. He and his wife planned to fertilize their sperm and egg in a test tube and then implant the embryo in a surrogate in Detroit. As a religious Jew, he would not proceed without approval from his rabbi, who ruled that Jewish religious ethics allowed and even encouraged birth surrogacy. I can envision similar questions to clergy in the near future as parishioners explore cloning humans as a strategy to overcome infertility. Unhesitantly, I would approve.

The Moral Questions Posed by Cloning

Cloning does present moral questions. Jewish ethicist Rabbi Elliot Dorff has pinpointed them. *"Who would be cloned?* If cloning is left to the economic forces of the marketplace, presumably the rich and famous, but not necessarily the good, would be cloned. This would exacerbate the socioeconomic divisions in society. . . . Human cloning may also be open to economic exploitation. A sports agent, for example, may seek to clone Michael Jordan to earn fees from many copies of him, presuming that human clones would have his athletic abilities."[4]

Second, *"how would the results of cloning be evaluated, and by whom? How would bad results be disposed of . . . ?* After all, good results would presumably be measured by the degree to which the clone matches the original, and that applies the standards of predictability and quality control—standards of industrial design—to human beings. This cheapens life, making human beings like inanimate objects on the assembly line. What may even be worse is the prospect of bad results. The sheep Dolly represents only one success out of two hundred seventy-seven attempts. Since human beings are even more complex organisms, we have every reason to believe that the technology needed to clone human beings will be every bit as inefficient, if not more so. What, then, will we do with the mistakes. Abort them? Kill them once born?"

And, last, *"to what uses would cloning be put?* The lure of cloning is that it holds out the potential for many good things. Scientists could learn much about the etiology and cures of diseases like cancer and Parkinson's, and the technique could be used to overcome infertility. Even these good uses have real risks. Human clones would have to have the protection of any other human subjects used in scientific research, and the children born through cloning must similarly be given all the same rights and protections of children born through sexual intercourse." These moral considerations argue for the regulation of cloning, not its banning.

Cloning Can Be Morally Acceptable

Rabbi Dorff argues that from a religious perspective, cloning, like other technologies, is morally neutral, depending on how it is used. Adam and Eve were put into the Garden of Eden "to work and preserve it." As long as a scientific technique is used to work and preserve the world, it is morally acceptable. At the same time, the Tower of Babel story warns us that we are not God, and that technology must be used with care, caution, and humility.

A potential benefit of cloning is to alleviate infertility, highlighted and stirred up by physicist Richard Seed, with his threat to open cloning clinics. Even though Seed has been portrayed as odd, his proposal is not immoral.

Pastoral counseling is a big part of a clergyperson's day. Bereavement is the most common and complex human situation that I counsel as a rabbi. The emotional despondency of infertility is a close second, and its sadness emulates bereavement. In bereavement after someone's death, one mourns what has been lost. Infertile parents mourn what has never been gained. A couple who has attempted unsuccessfully for years to conceive frequently suffers, as the mourner, feelings of frustration, blame, anger, and guilt. Both bereavement and infertility are about immortality. The inability to conceive offspring is to many like death without a body.

The Bible itself contains one episode after another of infertile couples. Abraham and Sarah cannot conceive until God "provides" a concubine with whom Abraham conceives Ishmael. Sarah remains barren through old age until through miraculous intervention she bears Isaac. Jacob bears a son with Leah, eliciting the envy of his preferred wife, Rachel, who is childless. Hannah prays and weeps because of her childlessness. Her husband, Elhanah, must assure her: "Am I not more to you than ten

179

sons?" The Bible's solutions for infertility may not be our twentieth-century solutions. But the clear message is that the Almighty laments childlessness and seeks solutions within nature and beyond. Cloning is one such natural solution that responds to the grief of God.

On the moral scale of the Talmud, when we improve the human lot in life we are "partners with God in creation." Other medical possibilities for cloning hold out the same potential for a positive partnership with God, but also require close monitoring. Treatment for cancer is one example, as is the transplant of a superfluous organ from the clone to a terminally ill sibling. Rabbi Dorff points out, for example, that "while it would be legitimate from a moral and Jewish point of view to produce a clone with the intent of transplanting bone marrow to an existing person with leukemia, it would definitely be illegitimate morally and Jewishly to produce the clone, perform the transplant, and then destroy the clone. Such organ harvesting must be prohibited if human cloning is to be allowed."[5] But these warnings argue for proper use of cloning, not its banning, in the same way that general organ transplant is carefully utilized, monitored, and regulated.

Unnecessary Religious Objections

Some of the common objections from religious spokespeople are, upon further reflection, unnecessary. "This is the playing of God by humans" is one such protest. I would ask those who raise this objection how they encourage any other means to repair faulty reproductive capacity, such as fertility drugs, artificial insemination, or in vitro fertilization? How, for that matter, do people of faith who hold such a position use chemotherapy to combat cancer, or even antibiotics to turn back what nature has decreed? With the exception of Christian Scientists and Catholics, in some instances (such as in vitro fertilizations), it is commonplace for people of faith to employ the healing measures as extensions of the biblical command to heal, and not as obstructions to the divine will. The double usage of the Hebrew root "rph" (רפא) in Exodus 21:19, usually translated as "He shall surely heal," is rather understood by rabbinic commentators to command the employment of God's healing in the first usage, and the capabilities and instruments of human healing in the second.

Still another contrary argument is that because cloning separates sex and reproduction, it ruptures the divinely intended tie between love and the conjugal act, and between parenting and family. But those in faith communities who have sexual relations while practicing birth control have already separated sex and reproduction. Natural parenting and reproduction have been differentiated in the case of adoption, itself a loving act in the Bible. Why do some suddenly protest cloning but not other cases in which parenthood is separated from conjugal sex?

Jewish biblical commentators see the three sons of Noah—Ham, Shem, and Japheth—as the progenitors of various races. Another concern is that the diversity of the human race which is intended in Genesis is aborted by the sameness that would be threatened by cloning. Apparently, this notion is a simplistic understanding of exactly what human cloning would produce. Silver explains that the essence of a cell's life may be contained within the cloned genetic material, but that the real core of human life—in the special meaning of the term—arrives on the scene at a later developmental stage. "Human life emerges only at a higher level, when trillions of cells in the brain all function together. The essence of human life lies within the human brain, not within inert molecules of DNA," he writes.[6] And that brain and personality develop not in response to a mechanistic cloning procedure, but in response to myriad life experiences, including interacting with culture, environment, religion, and other shapers of humanity in each of us. As with identical twins who, as life proceeds, may become very different in many aspects, so too differences between a clone and its "parent" are to be expected. The soul—the spiritual essence that transcends the physical—develops uniquely in each human being.

Religious People Should Embrace Cloning

Underlying the resistance of religious spokespeople to cloning is a more generalized resistance of religion to human technology, when the opposite should be the case. In the book *The Religion of Technology: The Divinity of Man and the Spirit of Invention,* David Noble argues that the technological enterprise has always been "an essentially religious endeavor." In the Middle Ages, monasteries served not only as the centers of worship but also as the matrix of inventions. The mechanical arts were not religion's enemies but its instruments, facilitating a return to a paradise of pre-Eden. Giordano Bruno, who stood at the threshold of modern science, regarded science as a catalyst for spiritual evolution. Newton wrote commentaries on Scripture. English scientist Robert Boyle wrote a book entitled *Some Physico-Theological Considerations About the Possibility of the Resurrection.* Charles Babbage, held to be the father of the modern computer, believed that advances in the mechanical arts constitute some of the strongest arguments in favor of religion.

In this century, inventor and artist Sam B. Morse, whose father was an evangelical founder of the American Bible Society, donated generously to religious organizations and sent as his first message, "What Hath God Wrought." The father of Orville and Wilbur Wright was a bishop of the Church of the United Brethren in Christ. Robert Thurston, first president of the American Society of Mechanical Engineers, thought that science and engineering were partners with "revelation and prophecy." Freemasonry, with its self-defined religious message, also was instrumental in spreading faith. Noble points out, "Masons have been among the most prominent pioneers of every American transportation revolution: canals (Clinton and Van Rensselaer); steamboats (Robert Fulton), railroads (George Pullman, Edward Harriman, James Hill); the automobile (Henry Ford), the airplane (Charles Lindbergh), and space flight (one half dozen astronauts)."[7] He shows that even atomic power once raised visions of both apocalypse and redemption.

The dawning technology of cloning to alleviate human suffering should also be embraced by formal religion. It enables couples who previously turned to anonymous strangers for egg, sperm, or embryo donations to have a genetic tie to their children and fulfill more directly the biblical mandate at Eden: "Be fruitful and multiply."

I disagree with my colleagues who support legislation to ban cloning. Science by its nature tells us the "how" of the world. Religion, by its nature, tells us the "why" of the world. Science explains the parts but cannot ascribe meaning to the whole. It can break down the components of one's body but not tell us whether the body should be bartered, prostituted, or killed by another or by one's self. It can tell us how to clone but not whether to clone. The input of classical religions and their spokespeople is needed to decide the moral acceptability of cloning. And religion's voice attests that carefully controlled cloning assists, rather than undermines, the Almighty.

NOTES

1. R. Albert Mohler, Jr., "The Brave New World of Cloning," in *Human Cloning: Religious Responses,* ed. Ronald Cole-Turner (Louisville: Westminster/John Knox Press, 1997), pp. 91-105.

2. Allen Verhey, "Theology After Dolly," *The Christian Century,* 19-26 March 1997, pp. 285-86.

3. John F. Hilner, "Stop Cloning Around: In the Flurry of Scientific Boundary Breaking, Let's Remember That Humans Are Not Sheep," *Christianity Today,* 28 April 1997, pp. 10-11.

4. This quotation and the two that follow are from Elliot N. Dorff, "Human Cloning: A Jewish Perspective," unpublished paper presented at the National Bioethic Advisory Committee, "Moral Issues" no. 3, 14 March 1997. The work was subsequently published in the University of Southern California Law School's *Interdisciplinary Law Journal,* vol. 8, no. 1 (Winter 1998): 117-29. Italics mine.

5. Ibid.

6. Lee Silver, *Remaking Eden: How Genetic Engineering and Cloning Will Transform the American Family* (New York: Avon Books, 1998), p. 236.

7. David Noble, *The Religion of Technology: The Divinity of Man and the Spirit of Invention* (New York: Alfred A. Knopf, 1998), as quoted in Edward Rothstein, "Technology," *New York Times,* 22 December 1997, sec. D, p. 3.

SHOULD HUMAN CLONING BE PERMITTED?

A *Response by* Abigail Rian Evans

I have the greatest respect for scientists and am opposed to knee-jerk reactions that treat scientific discoveries as somehow threatening rather than enlarging our understanding of the magnificent world that God has created. However, despite my respect for science, I oppose human cloning. My opposition is based on four principal reasons. Cloning (1) is not a necessary solution to any human tragedy, (2) fosters a reductionistic rather than a holistic view of human nature, while treating people as means rather than ends, (3) undermines the structure of the family, and (4) creates a pressure to use this technology and make it a god.[1] Further, grounds of my opposition are that it may (1) threaten the value placed on our individuality, (2) undermine the nuclear family by redefining human relationships, (3) be done for morally wrong motives, (4) further separate us from God the Creator, and (5) cause a loss of genetic diversity and a reduction of genetic sturdiness, which could adversely affect the human race.

Western civilization has experienced a shift from the Judeo-Christian concept of a God-centered universe to a nineteenth-century rationalism of a human-centered universe to a late–twentieth-century techno-centered world where science is harnessed to technology. Such a techno-centered worldview is illustrated by the descriptions used for the creating of human life—reproduction—a metaphor from the factory. *The question is how to reconcile a techno-centered worldview with theology.* Is cloning simply one more piece in the armamentarium of technological reproductive aids for childless couples, or is it a replication of a different moral order altogether?

It is with hesitancy that one opposes some of these reproductive technologies that may assist an imperfect nature in her job of providing couples with children, since there are ten million infertile couples in the U.S. today. Is resistance simply based on some romantic notion of parenthood and opposition to technology per se, or is it rooted in justified moral and religious reservations that cut at the very core of what it means to be human? If a good results, should the means be questioned? In our utilitarian-based society, outcomes normally trump, reinforced by our preferences for autonomy rather than duty-grounded morality.

What are the grounds for opposing human cloning, and should opposition lead to banning? How are hysterics on the subject of cloning avoided? The problem with the cloning debates is that they often take on preposterous proportions in the hands of science-fiction writers who describe multiple Hitlers and maleless planets. Even such reasoned columnists as Ellen Goodman in the *Boston Globe* referred to embryos appearing "in the freezer section of your bio-market."[2] This rhetoric is not helpful. In a recent poll, 91 percent of Americans said they would not clone themselves and 74 percent said it is against God's will.[3] When a 1993 *Time* CNN poll on opinions about cloning asked Americans, "Do you think human cloning is a good thing?" 14 percent said yes, and 75 percent no. The second question, "Would you like to have been a clone?" 86 percent said no, and 6 percent yes. Forty-six percent of the American public would make it a crime to clone a human.[4]

In addition, the scientific community has taken a cautious stance toward cloning. The American Medical Association's Board of Trustees called for a voluntary five-year moratorium by the medical and research community on cloning a human being. But, the board also said it supports research that is important to the health of patients, and urged Congress to write no legislation that would interfere with current human, animal, or cellular cloning-related research that is not directed at producing a human being.[5] It also called the procedure "morally unacceptable" at this time, but recommended a review within a three- to five-year period, at which time the technological situation should be reevaluated and the ethical and social implications reviewed.[6] The Society for Developmental Biology took a similar stance.[7]

Religious opinion on this issue is divided, with Roman Catholics at the conservative end. The Vatican L'Osservatore Romano even stated that cloning could lead humanity down "a tunnel of madness."[8] Richard McCormick, a Jesuit priest and professor of Christian ethics at the University of Notre Dame says, "I can't think of a morally acceptable reason to clone a human being."[9] Protestant ethicists such as Nancy Duff and Gilbert Meilaender represent different positions toward human cloning.

Before presenting the arguments against human cloning, some unfounded reasons for being opposed to human cloning will be discussed.

Unfounded Reasons for Being Opposed to Cloning

1. Let nature take its course. Finis Crutchfield, a former United Methodist bishop, said in 1993 that efforts to modify the work of the Creator constitute "pride, the deadliest of all sins."[10] However, we already "modify" nature, consuming genetically engineered milk, soybeans, and many other such foods. Many domestic plant and animal varieties have been produced by centuries of artificial selection by humans, that is, breeding. Human parts are replaced with animal ones in numerous surgeries, for example, pig valves. The success of modern medicine is built on "interfering with nature."

Having said this, however, from Jewish and Christian perspectives, humanity is commanded, on the one hand, to subdue the earth and, on the other hand, to be a steward of nature and her resources. Sin may overtake us; any procedure that is initially envisioned for good purposes can result in evil if it falls into the wrong hands.

2. Knowledge is dangerous—opening Pandora's box. The pursuit of knowledge is good; its application may not be.[11] The techno-centered worldview operates under the illusion that if there is a problem, science has the solution. However, technology may create its own problems. Perhaps one way of addressing the issue of cloning is to look at its application—good in plants, bad in humans—rather than condemning the procedure itself as wrong. Do the same moral judgments apply as those for nuclear fission, which was not intrinsically evil but rather produced evil when the atomic bomb was dropped? Or perhaps certain procedures should be prohibited because the dangers of their abuse are too great and people cannot be trusted to use them for good ends?

Solving problems of infertility is right and good, and improving crops and animals is part of our stewardship. Humans are responsible to know themselves and their world. The Human Genome Project already has made great strides at further unlocking the secrets of the wondrous ways that humans are made. Biologist Christopher Wills asserts the imminent discovery of the genes that contribute to intellectual ability and personality as well as those that determine manic depression or schizophrenia.[12] However, in analyzing the possibilities of producing a genius race, he goes to great pains to show this will not be possible, because approximately 10 billion harmful recessive mutations enter the human gene pool each generation to join those already present.[13] He also concludes that there are no bad genes, only bad alleles, which we can correct.[14]

With all its dangers, genetic research has the potential for tremendous good. One concrete illustration is its assistance in reducing prejudice based on faulty genetics. Repeated studies have shown that genetic differences between individuals chosen at random is far greater than slight differences between races. Racial differences have been shown to account for only 3 to 10 percent of genetic diversity harbored by our species.[15]

Knowledge is neutral and can be used for good or evil; we need not fear it. Theology does not stand against scientific insights, because God is one source of truth. This, it is hoped, provides some protection against prejudging what is acceptable science according to a narrow theology. Ignorance is not bliss.

However, in the instance of human cloning, randomized trials for cloning humans are not desirable. The research itself puts the subject at a greater risk than the potential benefit. What determines what is safe or unsafe? Although a moratorium has been called, what will come to light that will suddenly cause us to lift the moratorium? Cloning research has ethical implications as well as its application. The internal and external validity of cloning as a treatment is problematic at best. If cloning is the treatment, what is the disease? The issue at stake is the danger of the application of knowledge.

3. Cloned humans would not be unique. Religious leaders' opposition to cloning, according to Karen Lebacqz, is based on a perceived threat to our uniqueness.[16] Daniel Callahan, director emeritus of Hastings Center, an ethics-research organization, said people have a right to their own individual genetic identity, and cloning could well violate that right.[17]

Current genetics indicates, however, that the adult clone may physically be a replicate, but psychologically an entirely different person. The genotype is identical, but the phenotype is different. If one believes that each person is made in God's image as reflected in the soul, the soul is not a slot on a chromosome; it does not have a genetic makeup. The nature of our birth does not affect that fact. The nature of the soul is a theological, not a biological question, though one must avoid a Cartesian dualism. Since the soul is not genetic in origin, how could one's uniqueness be in peril?[18] Would the cloned individual somehow have difficulties entering fully into God's purposes? Every person is unique no matter the human method of birthing, because the ultimate creator is God.

There is no scientific basis for assuming that our psyches are copied along with our genes. DNA sequence analysis shows that the average person anywhere in the world is a 99.9 percent genetic copy of "me" and that humans share more than 90 percent of their genetic makeup with the chimpanzee. Furthermore, we have no difficulty in recognizing twins as unique human beings. A cloned individual is now being referred to as "noncontemporaneous twin."[19]

Reasons for Opposing Human Cloning

1. Cloning may threaten the value placed on our individuality. Cloned humans are unique persons, but cloning may force the individual to fulfill a predetermined destiny, so their psychological and spiritual individuality may be crushed. This is seen in a minor form when the football hero father disavows his artistic, nonathletic son, damaging the son's sense of worth and self-esteem. It is unknown how much power the progenitor will have over her clone. Will there be pressure to fulfill a preconceived destiny? Can one patent one's clone? Does it legally belong to the progenitor? If the cloned person views herself as an instrument of someone else's will, this could have disastrous results. One's dignity and value could be undercut.

Geoffrey Brown is concerned about the results, and bases his opposition on Barth's theology. The freedom for human self-determination is affirmed in Barth's concepts of care and love, finding its analog in the Trinity—three distinct persons related in love. Freedom for self-determination is to fulfill God's purpose for each individual. Brown argues that being a clone would limit human freedom, hence the ability to be an individual.[20]

2. Cloning may undermine the nuclear family by redefining human relationships. The Roman Catholic position states that most technical intervention is prohibited, including homologous artificial insemination by donor (AID), and the orthodox Jewish perspective goes further to say that AID is adultery. Given these views, then, the use of reproductive technologies becomes a moot question. Even if we do not agree with these perspectives, many people have a growing concern about our attitudes toward procreation—a separation of sex, love, and procreation where males become irrelevant. Humans may no longer view themselves as co-operating with a creator God, but with a sophisticated technology that creates babies from its test tubes. Birthing is no longer an outcome of an act of love between a husband and wife to bring a child into the world, but a laboratory experiment. Cloning humans raises perplexing questions: What is the meaning of parenthood? When should embryonic cells be considered a human life? How far should humans go in attempting to control their own destiny and designing their own progeny?[21]

There are several possible scenarios that illustrate the challenges to a family that human cloning would create. If a couple decide to create a clone because the mother is terminally ill, is there a danger the husband could fall in love with his daughter who looks like his wife? Or, if the wife miraculously recovers, is there a danger she would see herself displaced by her younger and healthier daughter? Is a woman's clone her daughter, her sister, or both, or a noncontemporaneous twin? If there were other children produced by "natural" means, how would they view their sibling? A cloned child may not be able to live up to expectations if the purpose was to replace a lost child. There could also be wrongful life suits by a cloned individual.

A cloned child may feel weaker links to both parents, especially with the father, who does not contribute anything genetically to the child. Although it is true that adopted children bond with their nonbiological parents, they also search aggressively for their biological parents. How would a child feel if there were no father to find?

3. Cloning may be done for morally wrong motives. Morally speaking, the agent's motives are as important as, if not more important than, the act. Hence the reasons for cloning become morally relevant. Most people would concede that producing a clone for the purposes of carrying forward a diabolical plot to kill thousands of innocent people would be morally reprehensible. Problems, for example, have already surfaced with uses of amniocentesis for sex selection by aborting the fetus. Whereas the presenting reason was to discover possible genetic anomalies, the real motive was sex selection. Cases such as the father who injected his son with the AIDS virus so that he would not have to make child support payments testify that truly evil motives are possible. Part of the concern about cloning is linked to views of human nature. Are humans free to do good, or are they predisposed to sin? If the latter, then the possibility of evil motives is strong, with little way to regulate against such motives that may remain hidden.

4. Cloning may further separate us from God the Creator. God as Creator is seen more and more as a quaint notion we left behind with a six-day creation story. Who needs God when we have the geneticist? It is true that

from the building of the Tower of Babel to Wall Street sky-scrapers, God persistently survives despite our attempts to make God unnecessary. According to annual Gallup polls over the past several decades, 90 percent of the American public continue to believe in God. However, reproductive technologies tend to separate us further and further from a creator God, a loving God, a parent God. Gilbert Meilaender's argument that a cloned child will be viewed as manufactured product instead of a gift from God carries moral weight.[22]

5. Cloning can cause loss of genetic diversity and reduction of sturdiness, which could adversely alter the human race. According to Eisenberg, wide-scale cloning would invite biological disaster. It would lead to a marked restriction in the diversity of the human gene pool, which would threaten the ability of our species to survive major environmental changes. (For this to happen, clones would need to exceed current numbers of in vitro fertil-ization births.) However, this reduction in genetic diver-sity will occur only if there is a selection of cloning with a bias toward certain genotypes. This has led as early as 1975 to the creation of "wild" species as a protection against catastrophe from new blights to which current high-yield grains prove particularly vulnerable.

Sexual-reproducing species greatly outnumber and outcompete asexual-reproducing species (only one thou-sand exist).[23] The inference is that sexual reproduction is a biological advantage in evolution. According to Eisen-berg, the benefit of sexual reproduction is the enhance-ment of diversity "by crossover between homologous chromosomes during meiosis and by combining the hap-loid gametes of a male and a female parent."[24] However, there are two principal theories as to why asexual repro-duction is inferior to sexual reproduction: (1) the accu-mulation of deleterious mutations in asexual reproduction, and (2) the inability to rapidly assemble new genetic combinations that are more fit in a changing environment.[25] Genetic diversity in both human and non-human species is a precious planetary resource, and it is in our best interest to monitor and preserve that diversity. Selecting traits that seem desirable in one moment of history is dangerous. Has nature built in warnings against this practice? As well, the cloned individual may age faster and be more disease prone. When a clone is taken from a thirty-year-old woman, is the clone "born" thirty years old? At this point we do not have the information about humans to categorically draw this conclusion.

In summary, with all the dangers and uncertainties that human cloning presents, I am opposed to proceeding with this procedure now or in the future.

NOTES

1. Abigail Rian Evans, "Saying No to Human Cloning," in *Human Cloning: Religious Responses,* ed. Ronald Cole-Turner (Louisville: Westminster/John Knox Press, 1997), pp. 25-34.

2. Center for Biotechnology Policy and Ethics newsletter, Institute for Biosciences, College of Liberal Arts, Texas A&M University, vol. 3, no. 4, 1 January 1994, p. 1.

3. Jeffrey Kluger, "Will We Follow the Sheep?" *Time,* 10 March 1997, p. 71.

4. Philip Elmer-Dewitt, "Cloning: Where Do We Draw the Line?" *Time,* 8 November 1993, pp. 65-70.

5. American Medical Association, "AMA Recommends Voluntary Moratorium on Human Cloning," AMA Web site *www.ama-assn.org/ad-com/releases/1998/980218a.htm.,* 17 February 1998.

6. American Medical Association, "Put Human Cloning on Hold, Say Bioethicists," *Medical News and Perspectives,* AMA Web site *www.ama-assn.org/sci-pubs/journals/archives/jama/vol_278/no_1/mn001301.htm.,* 2 July 1997.

7. Society for Developmental Biology, "Voluntary Moratorium on Cloning Human Beings," SDB Internet site *http://sdb.bio.purdue.edu/SDBNews/CloneRes.html.*

8. Elmer-Dewitt, "Cloning: Where Do We Draw the Line?" p. 65.

9. Richard McCormick, as quoted in Kluger, "Will We Follow the Sheep?" p. 70.

10. Richard N. Ostling, "Scientists Must Not Play God," *Time*, 20 June 1983, p. 67.

11. Paul Ramsey, *Fabricated Man: The Ethics of Genetic Control* (New Haven, Conn.: Yale University Press, 1970), pp. 122-23.

12. Christopher Wills, *Exons, Introns, and Talking Genes: The Science Behind the Human Genome Project* (New York: Basic Books, Harper Collins, 1991), p. 284.

13. Ibid., p. 310.

14. Ibid., p. 305. Note that some scientists would disagree with this position. See two Protestant ethicists' positions. Nancy Duff, "Clone with Caution: Don't Take Playing God Lightly," *Washington Post*, 2 March 1997, sec. C, pp. 1 and 5; and Gilbert Meilaender, "Begetting and Cloning," *First Things* 74 (June/July 1997): 41-43.

15. Ibid., p. 279.

16. Karen Lebacqz, "Cloning: Asking the Right Questions," *Ethics and Policy* (Winter 1997): 1, 5.

17. Elmer-Dewitt, "Cloning: Where Do We Draw the Line?" p. 68.

18. R. Geoffrey Brown, "Clones, Chimeras, and Barthian Bioethics," in *Bioethics and the Future of Medicine: A Christian Appraisal*, ed. John F. Kilner et al. (Grand Rapids: Eerdmans), pp. 238-49.

19. Robert Wachbroit, "Should We Cut This Out?" *Washington Post*, 2 March 1997, sec. C, p. 1.

20. Brown, "Clones, Chimeras, and Barthian Bioethics," pp. 238-49.

21. Shankar Vedantam, "Theologians Diverge on Human Cloning," *The Philadelphia Inquirer*, national, 15 March 1997, Web site *www.phillynews.com*.

22. Meilaender, cited in Jan C. Heller, "Religiously Based Objections to Human Cloning: Are They Sustainable?" in *Human Cloning*, eds. James M. Humber and Robert F. Almeder (Totowa, N.J.: Humana Press, 1998), p. 170.

23. Bernice Wuethrich, "Why Sex? Putting Theory to the Test," *Science*, vol. 281 (1998): 1980-82.

24. Ibid.

25. Ibid.

QUESTIONS

1. Are those who are involved in cloning research playing God with forbidden knowledge, or can they be considered cocreators with God?
2. Have these essays regarding cloning changed your perspective? If so, in what way?
3. Is it ethically desirable or feasible for human cloning to be prohibited?
4. If you had a child whose life might be saved by bone marrow from a cloned sibling, would you consent to the creation of that cloned sibling?
5. If human cloning becomes a reality, what role should communities of faith play in advocating that the technology is available to all and not just to those who can afford it?

CONCLUSION

TOWARD A THEOLOGY OF ASSISTED REPRODUCTION

Donald E. Messer

I
n response to the query "Does God care how we make babies?" the unmistakable and unequivocal answer echoes throughout history: Yes! The creation of new human life reflects both a divine mandate and a human responsibility in the continuous drama of existence. Celebrating and cherishing God's precious gift of procreation prompts persons of faith to affirm the mysteries of pregnancy and birth.

However, we now live in a new century, when medical technology permits one couple to make extra money by selling their sperm and ova to another couple. They purchase them so that they can have a "test-tube baby" produced at a clinic, and carried to term by a surrogate mother. When this happens, traditional Jewish and Christian understandings "of reproduction as a sacred act and union of the couple" cannot be fully appreciated or appropriated.[1] Welcome to a new world and moral future that challenges contemporary persons of faith to rethink their theological and ethical convictions.

For most of the past two Christian millennia, theological and ethical issues surrounding human procreation seemed rather clear and concise. Drawing from the book of Genesis, persons enthusiastically embraced the divine edict "be fruitful and multiply" (Genesis 1:28). The very term "procreation" means in Latin "to assist creation." Traditionally, the church only blessed married heterosexual persons having sexual intercourse in order to have babies. Masturbation, contraception, and abortion, for example, were ruled unethical and unacceptable not only by Catholics, but also by almost all Protestants until the latter began to change their teachings within the past fifty years.

Sex as Procreation and Re-creation

When sexual relations began being affirmed not only for human procreation but also as another form of human re-creation, revolutionary theological and ethical changes were prompted. Historically, from the time of Augustine, Christians emphasized the primacy of procreation and only secondarily the companionship value of "the unity of one flesh" in marriage. Basically, however, the proper purpose of sexual intercourse was to create children. Sixteenth-century Protestant reformers began to shift the emphasis more toward the affectional and companionship dimensions of marriage. But as contemporary persons of faith began to openly acknowledge the re-creational varieties of sexual pleasure and possibilities available to loving couples, new attitudes and perspectives emerged.

Jews and Christians, however, have never produced their own religious versions of the ancient Hindu *Kama Sutra*. The sensual Song of Solomon in the Hebrew Bible does not match the explicit sexual techniques and eroticism of the Hindu classic. Except for traditionally espousing a moral endorsement of heterosexual intercourse within the bonds of marriage, neither Jewish nor Christian communities have sought to articulate a comprehensive manual on the techniques of sexual intercourse or the art of lovemaking that might assist the reproductive process.

With the advent of modern reproductive technology, new worlds of science offered alternative avenues for creating babies rather than just the good, old-fashioned method of sexual intercourse. Infertile couples discovered new ways of making babies, thanks to artificial insemination of eggs by husbands, acquaintances, or strangers. Borrowed eggs from women, in vitro fertilization ("test-tube babies"), and even surrogate mothers emerged as real-life options and not science-fiction fantasies. To borrow Fredrick Abrams's colorful imagery, "the befuddled stork" (a mythic bird for mythic parents!) was caught in a complex web of unprecedented legal and moral issues unknown in previous generations of humankind. Previous religious and moral teachings floundered as legalized abortion, genetic engineering, and even human cloning emerged on an altered landscape of life.

Theological and Ethical Guideposts

If God cares about how we make babies, then what are the theological and ethical guideposts that ought to help persons of faith chart their way through this new frontier of assisted human reproduction? What are the key dimensions and dilemmas that Jews and Christians, and other persons of faith must address if we are to begin to understand the divine will and way for baby making in the twenty-first century? Is it simply a matter of rejecting the new options offered by medical science and labeling them immoral and inappropriate? Or shall we merely baptize every novel scientific development and quirky cultural innovation as a gift and blessing newly revealed by God? Can we make some reasoned, reflective ethical and theological judgments without simply sliding down a slippery slope into moral relativism and theological quagmires?

Confronting these and other questions, the authors in this book have staked out the basic guideposts essential to persons who wrestle with the critical ethical and theological axioms integral to the reproductive issues of conquering infertility, agonizing over abortion, and contemplating cloning. A synopsis of some of these conflicting insights and reasoned arguments follows in an attempt to help persons identify the critical considerations that must be faced in decision making and action-taking in this "brave new world" of baby making.

A Seamless Robe or a Coat of Many Colors?

In theological and ethical thinking, persons appreciate and applaud a coherent and cohesive system of beliefs and principles. How comforting to have clarity and ready-made answers to disturbing problems and predicaments. How assuring to know a map of right and wrong exists lest one get lost in the morass and jungle of contemporary life and culture. How distressing to realize that certain questions cannot be scientifically resolved and that shared moral consensus does not prevail either in society or in religious communities.

Thus a theological and ethical perspective that flows like a "seamless robe" has value and appeal.[2] Such a garment would fit any size, neither being suited for particular individuals or peculiar circumstances, nor being tailored for specific times or special cultures. Grounded in eternal truths, it claims to be the ideal for covering every circumstance and contingency, ensuring proper decision making and action taking.

In contrast, a theological and ethical "coat of many colors" suggests an appealing garment that stitches together various scientific and spiritual materials, with variations and nuances fitting the needs of individuals and circumstances.[3] Less certain about knowing God's will and way for the immediate moment and situation, it seeks to discern the right-making and wrong-making characteristics enmeshed in real-life struggles and issues. No less concerned with coherence and cohesiveness, it recognizes degrees of ambiguity and ambivalence that "seamless robe" theologians and ethicists dismiss or discount.

Traditional Sexual Ethics

Historically, in Western Christianity, the official teachings of the Catholic church on procreation, reproduction, and genetics have provided this "seamless robe" of theology, which has then been embedded in ethics and often in law. Drawing upon philosophical theories of natural law, human moral duties are said to derive from reasonable reflection on human nature. Built systematically from premise to premise, one conclusion leads automatically to the next. Once decided that the natural function of sexual organs and sexual intercourse is exclusively for purposes of procreation between married, heterosexual persons, then any other functional use or impediment of this natural function must be deemed immoral and against the intended will of God in creation. Prohibitions against masturbation, contraception, adultery, fornication, premarital sex, unmarrieds "living together," same-sex relationships, artificial insemination, in vitro fertilization, abortion, genetic engineering, and cloning emerge from these natural-law assumptions and doctrines. Like a "seamless robe," official Catholic papal proclamations seek to reflect a consistent theology and ethic articulating a Christian understanding that affirms life from the moment of fertilized conception. It makes no exceptions for other expressions of sexual desire or activity; it champions marriage and the family, guards against efforts to destroy human life in any form, and seeks to stop genetic tampering and potential cloning.

Of course, individual Catholics do not always follow the letter of the church law in regard to all of these teachings.

Catholic teachings have shifted since Vatican II, so companionship is now equal in importance to procreation. Theologians and ethicists "push the envelope" and discover nuances and possibilities probably not intended by the pope. Some bishops and priests have a pastoral way of responding to human issues of contraception and infertility that overlooks rigid prohibitions, or at least, overrides them with grace and forgiveness. Catholic laity do not march in lockstep with these teachings, as is evidenced, for example, by studies showing contraceptive use and rates of abortion among Catholics in some countries remains quite high, despite the strong antiabortion stance of the church.

Critics of natural-law approaches to theology and ethics note several objections. When rational, intelligent people reflect about human nature, they do not all reach the same conclusions. Therefore, because they do not agree about what human nature is, they end up with different moral theories derived from it. Human sexuality remains far more complex than determining that human genitalia were only created to be used for procreation and lovemaking between married human beings. The issue is whether these natural law axioms reflect Stoicism more than Christianity. Stoic philosophers first affirmed procreation as the only end justifying sexual passion; it was not a teaching of Jesus per se.

Since God alone is sacred, the processes of nature cannot be labeled inherently sacred and beyond human intervention. Both Jews and Christians can cite Scripture and traditions that undergird a theological understanding of humanity as cocreators with God. The medical enterprise of healing "natural" sicknesses and eliminating "natural" diseases reflects this cocreative responsibility with the divine. Helping human life flourish in the future certainly falls within this cocreator understanding.

Some authors in this volume represent, in general, the

"seamless robe" school of theological ethics. None of the authors strictly subscribes in all respects to the historic Catholic positions on reproduction and genetics, though some clearly have been deeply influenced by the rich traditions and thoughtful argumentation advanced by the Vatican through the centuries. The voices of evangelical Protestantism often overlap with Catholic perspectives. Thus, on individual issues, writers with sharply differing theological commitments reach similar, if not identical, moral judgments that would prohibit artificial insemination, in vitro fertilization, abortions, genetic designing of children, and cloning.

Contemporary Sexual Ethics

Other authors fit the "coat of many colors" description, since they draw the fabric of their materials from both Jewish and Christian Scriptures and tradition, but they sew their theological and ethical argumentation together with different stitches and with distinctive designs. With a primary focus on the individual's needs, along with the concerns for the family and community in which a person lives, they write of a life-centered moral theology that cautiously, but more readily, welcomes technological advances that are reshaping reproduction, the meaning of parenthood, and family. Because they accept the necessity of sometimes choosing between lesser evils, persons of faith are forced to live with tragic choices in a less-than-perfect world. In certain circumstances, and in light of special personal conditions, they say, yes, it is ethical to create babies using artificial insemination and in vitro fertilization, and that conscientious Jews and Christians can morally endorse abortion, genetic advances, and even cloning.

These theologians, ethicists, rabbis, and pastors emphasize a sexual ethic for Judaism and Christianity based, for example, on a broad interpretation of love within relationships. Sexuality reflects more than genital activity. The experience of sexual desire and pleasure represents a positive good, which serves both the procreation and re-creational interests of human beings and can be an avenue of ever deepening love and commitment. Marriage is affirmed normatively, and while procreation is celebrated, it is not deemed essential for wholesome relationships and marriage.

Critics of this style and stance of doing theological ethics worry that the exception becomes the rule, as individual situations triumph over consistent commitments to basic religious precepts and ethical principles. For example, because care and compassion toward persons suffering from infertility motivate the endorsement of reproductive techniques such as artificial insemination by donor strangers or in vitro fertilization using surrogate mothers, the bonds of parenthood and family weaken, and society stumbles into a frightening "brave new world" where almost anything technically possible becomes morally acceptable. Once late-term, partial-birth abortions, and selective abortions based on probable defects, disabilities, or diseases are ethically blessed, then the slide down the slippery slope to infanticide and eugenics appears inevitable. Religious individuals and communities must maintain traditional standards, even when the secular culture is hell-bent on societal destruction and disaster.

Of the authors in this book who can be classified within the "coat of many colors" school of theological ethics, none qualify as strictly situationalists. Rather, they attempt to develop a theological ethic that remains both faithful to their religious convictions and yet responsibly fits a given situation. They endorse, but almost always with serious qualifications and limitations, the ethical propriety and justification of test-tube babies, abortion, genetic engineering, and possibilities regarding cloning.

Key Questions to Be Addressed

By asking certain key questions that must be addressed in reflecting theologically and ethically on issues of reproduction and genetics, and ferreting out points of both agreement and disagreement among conscientious persons of faith, individuals can shape their own judgments and opinions on what is theologically appropriate and morally acceptable. What follows is an illustrative, not exhaustive, list of five queries essential for intellectual and spiritual exploration.

God's preferences? *First, does God have a preference how we make babies?* Without a doubt, the church traditionally has favored standard male and female copulation within a marital context. Without being so explicit, what has been endorsed is the loving insertion of the erect male penis into the receptive female vagina, and, presto, fertilization and implantation leading to pregnancy and birth. Any other form of baby making generally has been ruled out as sinful and unethical, and various types of penalties for crossing this norm have resulted.

Biblical records, however, provide more latitude in how babies have been created, seemingly with God's blessing. Especially the Hebrew Bible, or Old Testament as Christians call it, provides an interesting array of infertility stories about the struggles of barren women, including Sarah, Rebekah, Rachel, Hannah, and the wife of Manoah (Genesis 11:30, 25:21, 29:31; 1 Samuel 1:1-2; Judges 13:2). God apparently provides a concubine so that Abraham can conceive Ishmael. Sarah was barren until old age when she miraculously bears Isaac. Surrogate mothers are not contemporary innovations!

Except for the impregnation of the unmarried mother of Jesus, the New Testament is less illustrative of alternatives. Rather than dwelling on the particulars of sexual intercourse or the procreative process, New Testament

205

writers report a mixed, but generally positive, emphasis on marriage and the family, with denunciations of immoralities like sexual lusting, fornication, and licentiousness.

Of course, biblical writers and early church fathers did not anticipate or imagine the technological developments that would emerge at the end of the twentieth century that profoundly challenged and changed the possibilities of the baby-making process. Neither the Hebrew writers of the Talmud, or Protestant reformers like Martin Luther or John Calvin, could have foreseen the options of contraceptive pills, test-tube babies, genetic health testing prior to birth, or tampering with the human gene line. Thus we are left to speculating, and prayerfully considering, what the religious response of our spiritual foreparents might have been and what God might be revealing to us today.

Various theological treatises even have suggested that, despite the anonymity of sperm donation, the introduction of a "third party" is analogous to adultery. An ethicist like Paul Ramsey thought artificial insemination of a donor egg or creating life by in vitro fertilization would be tearing "radically asunder what God joined together in parenthood when He made love procreative."[4] The Vatican document *Donum Vitae* ("Gift of Life") states that "the procreation of a human person be brought about as the fruit of the conjugal act specific to the love between spouses."[5]

In contrast, ethicist Joseph Fletcher saw no justification for passively accepting infertility as God's will, arguing instead for new methods of assisted reproduction that helped persons escape biological determinism. Reproductive freedom and rationally planned pregnancies appeared natural for rational, hoping, thinking, and loving human beings.[6]

Probably no one would want to claim that biological

parenting is the only norm God endorses. Biblical witnesses often speak a concern for orphans, and persons of faith have long supported the practice of adoption. Many urge mothers of "unwanted children" to forgo abortion options, choosing instead to give them up for adoption because there are so many eager and excellent parents seeking to make a home for new babies. Complications abound in the adoption alternative, but clearly it is one established way of meaningfully caring for children and addressing the agony of childlessness.

While all the contributors in this book embrace the family unit for procreation and nurture of children, they divide on whether God has forever limited baby making to some first-century normative cultural pattern. Certain writers demonstrate degrees of openness to new procreative options made possible through scientific and technological breakthroughs. These innovations could be understood as forms of God's continuing revelation, and participation could mean joining cooperatively in God's endless creation adventure.

On the other hand, other authors hesitate to join quickly in the parade of promoters for the new procreation. For various reasons they hesitate to embrace wholeheartedly the new scientific technology lest, as Marilyn E. Coors suggests, they plunge down the slippery slope from approving "ethically questionable practices, such as the improvement of intelligence, . . . to other utilizations that are unethical, such as the practice of eugenics." Or, as R. Albert Mohler, Jr., warns: "Children are not the products of a technological process, like common consumer commodities, but are the gifts of a loving God whose intention it is that children should be born to a man and a woman united in the bond of marriage, and, as the fruit of that marital bond, realized in the conjugal act."

Loving alternatives? This leads to a second question: *Can alternative modes of procreation be expressions of loving* *relationships?* The positive bias toward traditional sexual intercourse for purposes of making babies makes it difficult for most of us to imagine that the use of medical techniques can be as emotionally and spiritually satisfying for infertile couples eager to have a baby. Without the loving passion of a marital bedroom, does having "test-tube babies" in this fashion become equivalent to shopping for some item in the public mall or neighborhood boutique?

Clearly the medical techniques are different, but they do not have to be unloving and uncaring. In fact, the reverse could be true. Celibate theologians of the past have gyrated about the pendulum from the extreme of tarnishing sexual intercourse as sinful to probably over-romanticizing the conjugal act's sweet spontaneity and joy! Persons yearning to have babies sometimes discover the regimen and routine of trying to get the fertile sperm connected with the mature ovum requires its own set of taxing disciplines and strenuous sexual acrobatics. Literally, being "up" for the sex act is not without its own marital tensions and troubles!

True, artificial insemination and in vitro fertilization can be cold, callous, impersonal, and unloving. Being forced to masturbate into a test tube in a doctor's bathroom while nurses and laboratory technicians await the results of ejaculation hardly feels romantic or even erotic. Likewise, a woman undergoing laproscopic procedures or other painful tests has to have the passionate desire of Rachel for motherhood when she cried in ancient Israel, "Give me children, or I shall die!" (Genesis 30:1).

In contrast, reports indicate that infertile couples hoping and praying to be parents can find the new procreative processes expressions and outlets of their love, tenderness, and care for each other. Using a syringe to help inject proper medication into your partner may sound like an unconventional act of love, but participants relate that it can be a moment of intimacy, as couples unite physically, psychologically, and spiritually in hopes of God's miracle of pregnancy.

Beginning of life? *Third, when does life begin?* Some questions reflect matters of value and judgment and cannot be verified by science. Primary among them stands the definitive question of when life begins. Medical authorities can speak to the query, but are unable to answer theological matters such as when personhood commences in the eyes of God. Likewise, no Bible references specifically address this subject.

Yet the answer to this inquiry decisively shapes a person of faith's moral response to almost all dimensions of assisted reproduction and cloning. The universal judgment of both Christians and Jews, and the foundation of contemporary legal systems, forbid the killing and destruction of human life. A shared religious conviction that human beings are created in the "image of God" means that persons should be protected, preserved, and prized. Anything harmful or contemptuous of human dignity and worth must be resisted and rejected.

But when does personhood begin? Theologian John B. Cobb, Jr., outlines six possible points when a fetus might have the essential characteristics of humanity. He notes that religious persons at various times have drawn the line at each of the following stages, because something significant happens developmentally at each of these stages: (1) a fertilized ovum, (2) a functioning brain, (3) implantation in the lining of the uterus, (4) viability—independence (real or potential) from the mother, (5) moment of birth, and (6) some later stage of maturation.[7]

The Catholic "seamless robe" ethic affirms life beginning with a fertilized ovum, and therefore its destruction, be it by some form of "morning after" contraception, abortion, selective reduction of zygotes during in vitro fertilization, or thawing and disposing of frozen embryos, is deemed explicitly evil and morally invalid. "Right to life" antiabortionists of all religious persuasions likewise are convinced that the potential life of a baby as represented by a fertilized ovum or fetus dare not be eliminated. Embryo extermination equals homicide.

Historically, Jews have revered and sanctified human life for nearly four thousand years. Anti-Semitism, fostered by Christians, contributed to the Christian Crusades, the Inquisition, and the systematic slaughter of six million Jews during the Holocaust. The Jewish people have experienced the evils of eugenics as practiced by the Nazis. They know and cherish life, yet they do not automatically oppose abortion, genetic engineering, or cloning, because Judaism generally has identified the moment of birth as the time a fetus is considered a person with rights.[8] Only theological and ethical "hubris," or unjustified pride and self-righteousness, could prompt Christians to call Jews "murderers" because Jews approve abortions prior to birth. Further, Jewish women are particularly susceptible to Tay-Sachs (a disease causing an agonizing and painful death of infants up to five years old), which is not detectable by amniocentesis tests until the second trimester of pregnancy. Thus preventive abortion may be deemed by Jews as a good, and potential genetic engineering that might eliminate this harsh disease a wonderful scientific advance in keeping with a loving God who wishes that evil be eliminated.

Christians employing a "coat of many colors" approach to theological ethics have profound respect for the human embryo as a potential person, but do not confer to the embryo at the time of biological fertilization the same rights and protection as possessed by a living person independent of the womb. With varying degrees of reluctance, Protestants approve of abortions, especially in cases when the physical and mental health of the mother and/or child is endangered, incest or rape has occurred, and prior to the point of potential independent viability.

Christian ethicists and church pronouncements generally deplore abortions prompted by concerns for personal convenience, as substitutes for contraception and population control, or for gender selection (for example, aborting healthy female fetuses). Rather than blanket condemnations of abortion and genetic engineering, mainline Protestants tend to focus on the plight of individuals in a less-than-perfect society and world.

The point of viability, when a child can live independently from the mother (with or without additional medical assistance), emerges as a widely accepted boundary. The legal line of twenty-three or twenty-four weeks of gestation will shorten as medical technology enables younger fetuses to be kept alive. The destruction of a more highly developed fetus is deemed a much greater loss than the discontinuation of a fertilized ovum.

Ironically, surveys indicate that Catholic women have about the same abortion rate as the national average, while Protestant and Jewish women have a rate about 30 percent below the national level. Evangelical or born-again Christian women reportedly have only half as high a rate of abortions as other religious and nonreligious people. As Martin E. Marty has noted, "If people in traditions that oppose abortions would stop having abortions, two-thirds or more of the abortions would end."[9]

The dilemma of a secular country like the United States, which champions religious freedom and respects religious pluralism, is reflected in the political polarization resulting from quarrels arising from the abortion debate. A total of 1,222,585 legal abortions were reported to the Centers for Disease Control in 1996.[10] Decades after the landmark Supreme Court decision in *Roe v. Wade*, public opinion polls demonstrate that the country still largely supports legalized abortions, though with a clear schism in the body politic. Public attitudes can be summarized as conditional acceptance, but with the hope that abortions should be "safe, legal, and rare." A "permit but discourage" model prevails.[11]

No law or policy can completely embrace the multiplicity of deeply held opinions regarding when life begins and the moral justifiability of abortion. Perhaps the best it can do is to ensure that no one is forced to have an abortion and to set reasonable medical and legal standards regulating its use. The Supreme Court in 1973, in *Roe v. Wade*, reflects such an attempt, but obviously conscientious proponents of a total ban on abortion will never quit challenging its provisions. If *Roe v. Wade* were overturned or changed, other conscientious persons of faith would assert that their individual freedom and personal consciences were being violated.

New complexities continue to emerge and are still being pondered by the public and tested in legislatures and courts. Illustrative are the policy debates regarding late-term, or "partial-birth," abortions that have taken center stage in recent years. The procedure is relatively rare, but many persons generally supportive of abortion as necessary for reproductive freedom have expressed strong reservations about this seemingly gruesome procedure that borders on infanticide.[12] It is hoped that the debate between Tex Sample and Joan Winfrey in this volume will enable readers to think through this "hot button" political and moral issue.

Another perplexing quandary is what to do with the more than one hundred thousand frozen embryos stored in fertility clinics around the United States. Reportedly, one-fifth of the embryos are involved in some type of dispute, so they reside in "legal limbo"—a new type of purgatory for those who equate them with personhood. Clear policies and consistent guidelines for their use and/or disposal generally do not exist.

Easy answers may exist for some people regarding the dispute over when life begins, but general consensus as to what is right or wrong, good or evil, remains elusive and challenges every person of faith to make a conscientious decision based on prayerful reflection on basic theological and ethical commitments.

Benefits? *Fourth, what benefits result from employing these new possibilities in reproduction and genetics?* Doing good and avoiding evil—helping and not harming persons—serve as moral bedrocks in religious, medical, and legal communities. Whether it is the commandment ("You shall not murder"), the physician's Hippocratic oath ("First, do no harm"), or the philosopher's principles of beneficence and nonmalfeasance, the burden of proof always weighs heaviest in the direction of ensuring the life and well-being of the person. Sometimes choices are crystal clear in terms of right and wrong, but other times persons must consider and weigh the preponderance of benefits versus harms, and vice versa. Within these "gray" areas of life, where ambiguity reigns, persons of faith must struggle to discern what is actually best or more right-making.

Assisting reproduction through medical technology clearly produces some desirable benefits to individuals, families, and society. Six million American women suffer infertility, an increase of 25 percent over the last decade. One can quantify neither the sorrow and pain of infertility nor the stress it causes couples, nor the great joy, happiness, and lifelong satisfaction that comes with parenting a child. Barrenness and sterility often can be profound personal dilemmas that threaten self-worth and meaning for many persons. One cannot underestimate the genuine fear of the "biological clock running out" for a woman before she can give birth to a healthy child. Age forty may or may not be too old to bear a child or care for one, but often, due to "old eggs," it becomes too late to conceive a baby.

Infertility represents a recurrent biblical theme with contemporary overtones. Ancient Israelites "regarded

213

their God as the giver or withholder of children."[13] Many, therefore, can identify with the depression and "sad heart" of Hannah, who described herself as a "woman deeply troubled" with "great anxiety" as she struggled against infertility and yearned for a child. After her prayers were answered, she conceived and bore a son, naming him Samuel, "for she said, 'I have asked him of the LORD' " (1 Samuel 1:1-20). Sometimes Samuel's name is translated from Hebrew to mean "God has heard."[14]

Many persons of faith today feel that their prayers are being answered in the new medical movement to conquer infertility. God has heard and is working through scientists and physicians to remove impediments to fertility and to create new ways for making babies. As religious persons, they welcome developments ranging from artificial insemination (by spouse or donor), in vitro fertilization, possible genetic engineering interventions for health reasons, and potentially even cloning that might create a "twinned" child of the mother. Families, for example, have benefited by artificial insemination by way of donors, thus avoiding the transmission of genetic diseases or disorders (especially when both parents carry a recessive gene).

Genetic engineering promises genetic detection that might predict risks of alcoholism or eliminate possibilities of hemophilia being transmitted to the next generation. Ethicist Ronald Cole-Turner reports that, thanks to the federally funded Human Genome Project, more diseases in the future will be predictable and more pregnancies will be screened. The ability to predict a horribly painful life adds to the abortion debate. When, asks Cole-Turner, is "predicted suffering so intense, when is a life so distressful, and when is its toll on a family so unbearable that the continuation of a pregnancy is best avoided?"[15]

Beginning with Louise Brown, who was born on July 25,

1978, up to three hundred thousand babies were born by way of in vitro fertilization globally in the first twenty years. Brown's twentieth birthday was celebrated in England's House of Commons with a party attended by other "test-tube babies" and their parents. In 1998, a forty-four-year-old California woman gave birth, thanks to embryos that she and her husband had frozen eight years previously. A year earlier, many an eyebrow was raised and heads shaken when a sixty-three-year-old woman gave birth using donor eggs. On the other hand, great joy was expressed when newspapers and television screens pictured an Oklahoma City couple holding their new baby as a result of in vitro fertilization. She had chosen to have a tubal ligation after their second child had been born, but then their two children were killed in the terrorist bombing of that city's federal building. In the mother's words, "We were all excited . . . a new beginning for everybody."[16]

Harms? *Fifth, the benefits of these new developments, however, must be measured and weighed against risks and harms inherent in the processes.* Unfortunately, it is not always a joyous "new beginning for everybody." "Progress" against infertility is not an unblemished ethical good, but includes certain moral downsides that threaten the health and well-being of mothers, children, and families. We must explore whether the good gained exceeds the worth of risks taken and the losses suffered. Even strict utilitarian ethicists have to ask whether "the greatest good for the greatest number" is actually being served by these medical developments. A partial list of ethical objections and concerns can be listed:

(a) Questions of health and the well-being of women must be addressed. Invasive medical procedures are not without pain and suffering to women. The possibilities of success are still quite limited, with estimates ranging from 15 to 25 percent. The risks of overstimulating ovaries and awakening future ovarian cancer must be acknowledged.[17] Whether women who have had one or more abortions later suffer more frequently from problems of infertility has been raised but not conclusively answered.

Using surrogate mothers especially presents a perplexing ethical situation. Unusual and tender stories periodically appear about how a close relative bears the child for an infertile couple. Besides messing up traditional family structures, situations like this raise unresolved issues about the social/psychological effects on the identity of the child and family. The question remains whether the surrogate woman is being exploited. H. Tristram Englehardt, Jr., poses a tough question when he asks, "Is the woman exploited who is hired by an affluent couple to function as a surrogate mother, or is the woman exploited by those with special moral intuitions who use the law to stop her from hiring herself out as a surrogate mother and thus restrict the range of her choices?"[18]

My mother, and other women farmers I knew, used to talk about the "egg money" they earned by selling the eggs of their poultry. In a bizarre twist, today when women speak of "egg money," they are more likely conversing about selling their good ovarian eggs so that some other woman can produce a baby. Recently, advertisements have been placed in Ivy League college newspapers offering to pay $50,000 plus expenses for a tall, smart, athletic woman's eggs. Very specifically, the donor is to be at least 5 feet 10 inches tall, with a minimum SAT score of 1400, and no family medical problems.

Governments restrict sales of human organs, believing they take unfair advantage of human suffering for financial reasons. Current laws permit sales of sperm, ova, and the collection of endless medical and legal fees. Everybody but the surrogate mother gets money in the process. Columnist Susan Estrich asks rhetorically, "If men could bear children, would they pass laws saying that it could only be done for nothing?"[19]

(b) Long-term health consequences for cloned or "test-tube babies" remains quite unknown. It would be ethically prudent to attempt to calculate the manifest and latent consequences of likely social and personal changes that might result from redesigning human nature, even when the intent is good, such as removing undesirable genes.

Another question would be how long should specialists work to save the life of a "preemie" who weighs little more than a pound and probably will suffer lifelong health problems if he or she survives? Multiple, low-weight births commonly occur due to in vitro fertilization. Some studies suggest babies born this way may be exposed to greater possibilities for disease and deformities. Only Australia has kept consistent statistics of children born as a result of in vitro fertilization. Their preliminary studies suggest, "These children are two or three times more likely to suffer such serious diseases as spina bifida and transposition of the great vessels (a heart normality)."[20] As Cynthia B. Cohen notes, "If it were known in advance that children conceived with the assistance of the new reproductive technologies would not have an adequate opportunity for health, it would be wrong to use them." Lest that be misinterpreted, she further asserts, "It is not the children we disvalue, but the disorders that they have sustained. Consequently, it is not necessarily a reproach to disabled children who are already born if decisions are made against knowingly conceiving children who would have the same disabilities."[21]

Technology often stimulates the "revenge of unintended consequences" because unforeseen problems arise. Some scientists suspect in vitro pregnancies may result in a greater frequency of "chimeric hermaphrodite" children, having both male and female sex organs. Chimerism may be a good reason to limit the number of embryos transferred during in vitro procedures.[22] Higher rates of multiple births *in vitro* contribute to more preterm and low birth-weight babies. Children conceived this way thus are subject to higher incidence of perinatal, neonatal, and infant mortality. Parents must be fully informed of the risks that these new scientific techniques present to the mother, future child, and family.

Human cloning appears inevitable. Exactly when it will happen, no one knows. Fear has been expressed that there will be increased risks of birth defects in children brought to term. Cloning experimentation poses great risks. Temptations to clone individuals to serve as sources for transplantable organs will exist. H. Tristram Engelhardt, Jr., warns:

> As we develop our capacities to engage in genetic engineering not only of somatic cells but of the human germline, we will be able to shape and fashion human nature in the image and likeness of goals chosen by human persons, not by nature or God. In the end, this may mean so radically changing human nature that our descendants may be regarded by subsequent taxonomists as a new species.[23]

(c) What happens to unused fertilized embryos poses serious ethical problems. For those convinced these zygotes are potential persons and thus have the same rights as living human beings, this issue gravely compromises their own sense of right and wrong. If conservative religious people agree to the destruction of these embryos, they are participating in a "prenatal massacre." If they leave them suspended in frozen state, they have suspended thousands of unborn babies indefinitely between heaven and hell. If they attempt to find surrogate mothers for all these embryos, they have endorsed medical procedures they have previously deemed evil and immoral. Other persons of faith, who may not believe that zygotes are fully human beings with the same rights and status, still are conscientiously troubled with this dilemma, as they do not care to be callous about potential life or dismiss cells as worthless, or fetuses as simply tissues to be discarded.

(d) Outrageous and excessive worst-case scenarios cannot be ignored. Perhaps these reflect the price of living in a free society, but religious conservatives have valid concerns about how the culture and society are being reshaped and what type of future civilization will exist.

"Posthumous pregnancies," which take the sperm from a dead man to impregnate a widow, may in individual cases bring happiness. But is it really in the best interests of family life and societies that death provides no barrier to producing children and grandchildren one has never had? A clinic in California sought to collect the sperm of only very intelligent men, preferably Nobel prize winners. No contemporary religious ethicist—Catholic, Protestant, or Jewish—supports eugenics that seeks to take selected sperm or egg simply to create designer children, to eliminate sexual orientation, or to choose the gender of one's baby.

Beware, however, of making ethical decisions based on misinformation or fantasies inspired by science fiction. Our images of cloning often spring from seeing movies like *Boys from Brazil* rather than studying molecular biologist Lee M. Silver's book, *Remaking Eden: Cloning and Beyond in a Brave New World,* or philosopher Gregory E. Pence's edited volume called *Flesh of My Flesh: The Ethics of Cloning Humans.*[24] Clones are not robots or automatons, but identical twins separated in time by birth. Cloned persons, however, would have distinct personalities, shaped not only by their genes but also by their nurturing environment. It will not be possible to clone baptized and born-again Christians demonstrating the marks of true redemption and sanctification!

Our image of wicked governments making clone soldiers or slaves distorts the real value and meaning of cloning developments and their potential for human good. Protection of human safety and values ought to be the primary concern of persons of faith as we contemplate the new world emerging in the twenty-first century.

(e) Questions of justice and stewardship in the distribution of health resources must be faced. The procedures in question are extremely expensive and thus become the prerogative of the rich, not the poor, in any given society. The cost of cloning will be enormous, and thoughtful persons of faith must ask whether God really wills such extreme expenditures. If cloning becomes commercialized, possibilities for abuse abound.

We need to re-ask the age-old biblical question of what does the Lord require of us. Does doing justice, loving mercy, and walking humbly with God permit us to endorse any expenditure for genetic engineering or cloning? Or does it make a difference what we spend for these services in light of the fact that we live in a world where children still starve; live abandoned in orphanages in eastern Europe, China, and elsewhere; and die daily from diarrhea and other curable maladies such as cholera and tuberculosis that could be cured or curbed by applying additional monies.

No Easy Ethical Answers

No easy answers or simple magic markers denote what is more right and more wrong. Sometimes, based on ethical and theological reflection, we say both yes and no. We choose to draw lines beyond which we cannot conscientiously go. Affirmation of life might mean endorsing artificial insemination, limited use of abortion, controlled efforts at in vitro fertilization, but then saying no to genetic engineering or cloning that attempts to go beyond improving health and eradicating diseases.

As with many other human choices, the axiom remains that what is legal may not be ethical, and all that is moral ought not be enacted into law. Persons of conscience have to choose behaviors and set limits beyond which they will not ethically go.

Living in a secular, pluralistic society where no moral vision is shared means sometimes being supportive of policies and practices that personally one does not endorse. Personally, I might deplore abortion but support the constitutional right for a woman's right to choose. Respectful of the religious consciences and the right of people to be free from religious restraints means functioning as a personal witness to certain values that are not embraced by the culture and society as a whole.

Bioethicists and hospital chaplains often are called upon professionally to help strangers struggle with moral and theological issues. They may or may not share the same value and faith commitments as those they counsel. Chaplains and bioethicists should not be "ethics police," but rather should assist people in their own decision making. The decisions persons legitimately reach can be quite contrary to the professional's personal point of view. For example, bioethicist H. Tristram Englehardt, Jr. (who describes himself as "a born-again Texan Orthodox Catholic"), writes:

> I am of the firm conviction that, save for God's mercy, those who willfully engage in much that a peaceable, fully secular state will permit (e.g., euthanasia and direct abortion on demand) stand in danger of hell's eternal fires. . . . Though I acknowledge that there is no secular moral authority that can be justified in general secular terms to forbid the sale of heroin, the availability of direct abortion, the marketing of for-profit euthanatization services, or the provision of commercial surrogacy, I firmly hold none of these endeavors to be good. These are great

moral evils. . . . To be free is to be free to choose very wrongly.[25]

Yes, all of us run the risk of making the wrong decisions. If we follow a strict ethical principle or system of rules, we presumably have the possibility of being right some, maybe even most of the time. However, if we judge situations or issues case by case, realizing that principles are often in conflict and one must sometimes choose between evils, we run the risk of being wrong all of the time. There is no assurance in making decisions about reproduction that one is ever absolutely right.

Thus as a religious person, one lives with faith and hope, and above all, with grace, trusting in God's forgiveness and understanding. I affirm with my colleague and coeditor, Sally B. Geis, that "what we encounter in the living of life is not disembodied principles, but rather human beings who struggle mightily with the reality of their situations, often seeking to do what is right, yet discovering that they are torn by conflicting possibilities."[26]

We seek a life-centered theological ethic, trusting in the mercy of God. Such an ethic would be informed but not restricted by arbitrary moral codes or religious rules that fail to struggle with personal and social realities. Ready-made theological answers to complex ethical choices do not exist, and we are forced to pray and think as faithfully and thoroughly as we can.

Understanding our calling to be cocreators, coworkers, and co-explorers with God is not without risks, theologically and ethically.[27] This does not mean attempting to "play God" or assume the divine role in human history. Rather, one seeks to discern where God's liberating and loving initiatives are manifest in the world, and then join cooperatively in those processes.

God, along with scientists, medical technicians, ethicists, and others, is creatively working on the human frontiers of reproduction and genetics. The human capacity to control procreation reflects the freedom and powers of reason that God has given us. We do not simply passively receive ancient religious teachings, like the so-called natural law, but test and reappropriate their truths in light of new scientific and cultural understandings.[28] Using the new reproductive technology not for self-indulgence or selfish purposes, but in the service of God's intent for health and the well-being of all creation will be our continuing challenge.

An Open Letter to My Grandchildren

This book begins with a dedication to my grandchildren, Rachel and Noah, and ends with unsolicited advice to them and their future siblings or cousins. In this open letter to my beloved grandchildren, I reveal my own theological and ethical assumptions, perspectives, and hopes about how all persons of faith might flourish faithfully and fruitfully in the amazing new reproductive and genetic world of the twenty-first century.

With Carl Sandburg I would affirm that "a baby is God's opinion that the world should go on." Constant social changes and challenges, along with personal pressures and problems, prompt us all periodically to shout, "Stop the world; I want to get off!" But then with the birth of a baby, we are reminded of God's great blessings and the joy of living.

Unfortunately, Jews and Christians are divided on many topics, but on one matter they are and always have been united: Human beings should strive for a world in which every child is treated as a special gift of God. Each person is unique, made in the image of God, whether through natural procreation processes or by new technologies of reproduction. Every person is to be cherished and valued and loved unconditionally.

What I would hope for you, my grandchildren, I would also wish for others in this world. Speaking specifically of sexuality and reproduction, I pray you will be free to affirm your God-given sexual identity. Whether you be heterosexual or homosexual, may you know yourself as a cherished child of God, and may you live in a culture and a country that respects your differences and your rights as a human being.

Remember that sex and sexuality are good gifts of a caring God to be used, not abused or misused, for self-expression, loving relationships, marriage, and procreation. I pray someday you too will share in the magnificent mystery and glory of pregnancy and parenthood. May you not have to share the anguish of infertility and barrenness, but if that should arise, I trust all of the options, from adoption to insemination to in vitro fertilization to genetic engineering and cloning, are readily available to assist you in your quest. May you feel such a journey to procreation and parenthood is not a secular, but a spiritual adventure you and your beloved partner share as cocreators, coworkers, and co-explorers with God.

May the legal alternative of abortion exist, but with all my heart and soul I hope you will never find it a necessary choice. May it always be an option of last resort. I deplore the high rate of current abortions, and trust those numbers will decrease in the years ahead. But life is complicated, hard, ambiguous, and full of surprises, and we never know when we or loved ones might have to make hard choices due to unexpected circumstances.

Restrain, however, your judgment of others who may not see or experience these matters in the same way. Be both pro-life and pro-choice, affirming the special, almost sacredness, of human life, and yet also championing individual freedom and human rights. Every abortion represents to some degree a tragedy to be mourned. Let us, therefore, not be judgmental about those who conscientiously choose abortion, but let us be compassionate, not burdening them with unnecessary guilt that only compounds their grief. Truly may abortions be safe, legal, and rare.

You are going to be living in an expanding world of options and choices about procreation and parenthood. Life is a choice of values. Neither accept nor reject too readily every new scientific medical development. Measure them carefully, checking out the benefits and harms to mothers, infants, family, and society. Ask about the long-range health consequences of genetic engineering and cloning. Endorse that which promises good, and resist that which promotes evil. Do not foreclose your mind about positive dimensions of cloning, but be politically vigilant against inappropriate efforts to tamper with genetic structures and germ lines. Neither panic about the dangers, nor pretend all that emerges represents a great good.

In closing, let me say that I believe God does not care so much how we make babies, but that we lovingly care for the babies we help make. Remember that no matter how a child is conceived, a baby is a precious gift and blessing of God to be cherished and adored. Work for a world where every child is wanted and protected and enabled to flourish to her or his full potential. May you embrace a theological ethic that is not dysfunctional to life, but rather enables you to exhibit and experience God's grace while making reflective ethical decisions and taking responsible actions.

NOTES

1. H. Tristram Englehardt, Jr., *The Foundations of Bioethics*, 2d ed. (New York: Oxford University Press, 1996), p. 277.
2. The late Cardinal Joseph Bernardin developed the "seamless gar-

ment" argument, noting that if the Catholic position on the sacredness of life is to be taken seriously, its implications must be evident in terms of abortion, assisted suicide, war, capital punishment, and care for the poor. See Joseph Bernardin, "A Consistent Ethic of Life: An American-Catholic Dialogue," speech delivered on 6 December 1983 at Fordham University. Also see *The Seamless Garment* (Kansas City: National Catholic Publishing, 1984), pp. 3-8.

3. The King James Version of the Hebrew Bible declares that because Israel loved his son Joseph more than any of his other children, Israel gave him "a coat of many colors" (Genesis 37:3). Subsequent biblical revisions (RSV and NRSV) translate the garment to be "a long robe with sleeves." Contemporary religious and cultural presentations like Andrew Lloyd Webber's "Joseph and the Amazing Technicolor Dreamcoat" have retained the popular imagery of a coat of many colors.

4. See Paul Ramsey, *Fabricated Man* (New Haven: Yale University Press, 1970), p. 39.

5. *Sacred Congregation for the Doctrine of the Faith, Instruction on Respect for Human Life in Its Origin and on the Dignity of Procreation* (Vatican City, 1987), pp. 28-30.

6. Joseph Fletcher, "Ethical Aspects of Genetic Controls," *New England Journal of Medicine* 285 (30 September 1971): 776-83; *The Ethics of Genetic Control* (Garden City, N.Y.: Doubleday Anchor, 1974); *Morals and Medicine* (Princeton, N.J.: Princeton University Press, 1954).

7. John B. Cobb, Jr., *Matters of Life and Death* (Louisville: Westminister/John Knox Press, 1991), p. 80.

8. See excerpts of the testimony by Rabbi Balfour Brickner on behalf of the Religious Coalition for Abortion Rights before the Subcommittee on Civil and Constitutional Rights of the Committee on the Judiciary, U.S. House of Representatives, 24 March 1976.

9. Martin E. Marty, *Context*, 1 January 1989, p. 5. See also *Context*, 1 October 1997, p. 6; and "Catholics and Abortion," *The Washington Post National Weekly Edition*, 24-30 October 1998, p. 38.

10. Women who obtained legal abortions in 1996 were predominately white, under twenty-five, and unmarried. About one-fifth of the women were adolescents. More than half (55 percent) of legal abortions were performed during the first eight weeks of pregnancy; approximately 88 percent were performed during the first twelve weeks of pregnancy. Approximately two-thirds of women having abortions plan to have children in the future. The number of abortion providers in the U.S. decreased by 18 percent from 1982 to 1992. No abortion providers exist at all in 84 percent of U.S. counties.

11. See *New York Times* poll reported in *the Orlando Sentinel*, 16 January 1998.

12. For example, New York Senator Daniel Patrick Moynihan, who traditionally supports a woman's right to choose, described "partial-

birth" abortion to be "as close to infanticide as anything I have come upon." Infanticide historically was practiced throughout the world both to dispose of newborn babies and to control population growth. Wide acceptance existed in the Greco-Roman world. Plato endorsed it, and Aristotle wrote in his *Politics*: "Let there be a law that no deformed child shall live." Christians strongly condemned infanticide. The Didache, for example, declared, "Thou shalt not procure abortion, nor commit infanticide." For a legal discussion of "partial-birth" abortion, see George J. Annas, "Partial-Birth Abortion, Congress, and the Constitution," *The New England Journal of Medicine*, vol. 339, no. 4 (23 July 1998): 279-83.

13. Trevor Dennis, *Sarah Laughed: Women's Voices in the Old Testament* (Nashville: Abingdon Press, 1994), p. 120.

14. See Anita Diamant, *The New Jewish Baby Book* (Woodstock, Vt.: Jewish Lights Publishing, 1994); and Alan Benjamin, *A Treasury of Baby Names* (New York: Signet Books, 1983). Proper translation, however, is a matter of dispute among scholars. See, for example, Dennis, *Sarah Laughed*, p. 189 n. 22.

15. Ronald Cole-Turner, "Religion and the Human Genome," *Journal of Religion and Health*, vol. 32, no. 2 (Summer 1992): 166.

16. George Lane, "Mom Who Lost Two Boys in Blast Welcomes Third," *Denver Post*, 13 January 1998, sec. A, p. 10.

17. See Liz Tilberis, *No Time to Die* (New York: Little, Brown, and Company, 1998).

18. Engelhardt, *The Foundations of Bioethics*, p. 276.

19. Susan Estrich, "Egg Money," *Denver Post*, 8 March 1999, sec. B, p. 7. She is paraphrasing a cynical bumper sticker that reads: "If men could get pregnant, there would be an abortion clinic on every corner."

20. See Cynthia Cohen, "Give Me Children or I Shall Die! New Reproductive Technologies and Harm to Children," *Hastings Center Report*, March-April 1996, p. 20.

21. Ibid., p. 26.

22. Rick Weiss, "Test-Tube Baby Born A Hermaphrodite," *Denver Post*, 22 January 1998, sec. A, p. 20.

23. Engelhardt, *The Foundations of Bioethics*, p. 413.

24. See Lee M. Silver, *Remaking Eden: Cloning and Beyond in a Brave New World* (New York: Avon Books, 1997); and Gregory E. Pence, ed., *Flesh of My Flesh; The Ethics of Cloning Humans: A Reader* (Lanham, Md.: Rowman & Littlefield, 1998).

25. Engelhardt, *The Foundations of Bioethics*, p. xi.

26. Sally B. Geis, unpublished lecture, Luther Academy, June 1996, p. 3.

27. See Ronald Cole-Turner, "Is Genetic Engineering Co-Creation?" *Theology Today*, p. 348.

28. This position parallels how Chrysostom Zaphiris describes Eastern

Orthodox thinking. He writes: "Thus natural law, according to Eastern Orthodox thinkers, is not a code imposed by God on human beings, but rather a rule of life set forth by divine inspiration and by our responses to it in freedom and reason." Chrysostom Zaphiris, "The Morality of Conception: An Eastern Orthodox Opinion," *Journal of Ecumenical Studies* 11 (1974): 688.

QUESTIONS

1. Does God care how we make babies?
2. Does God have a preference for how we make babies?
3. Can alternative modes of procreation be expressions of loving relationships?
4. What benefits and what harms may result from employing these new possibilities in reproductive technology and genetic manipulation?

GLOSSARY

Editors' Note: Most definitions can be found in *Stedman's Medical Dictionary*, 24th ed. (Baltimore: Williams & Wilkins, 1982). Some of the terms used in recent articles about cloning were defined in *Update*, vol. 14, no. 2, Loma Linda University Center for Christian Bioethics, July 1998, p. 3.

abortion Giving birth to an embryo or fetus prior to the stage of viability at about twenty weeks of gestation (fetus weighs less than 500 grams). *Stedman's Medical Dictionary* lists twenty-four varieties of abortions; for example, complete; incipient (where there is copious vaginal bleeding, uterine contractions, and cervical dilation); incomplete, in which part of the products of conception have been passed but part (usually the placenta) remains in the uterus; spontaneous (commonly called *miscarriage*); and induced and therapeutic, to save life/preserve health of the mother.

AID An artificial insemination donor.

allele One of the alternative forms of a particular gene. Each gene of an organism can exist in slightly different forms. These small differences are responsible for some of the variations observed in different individuals within natural populations. Different alleles for genes that produce the blood protein hemoglobin, for example, will affect how well the blood cells will carry oxygen.

amniocentesis The surgical insertion of a hollow needle through the abdominal wall and uterus of a pregnant female, especially to obtain amniotic fluid for the determination of sex or chromosomal abnormality.

cervix The neck of the uterus and the opening from the vagina into the uterus.

chromosome One of the bodies (normally forty-six in humans) in the cell nucleus that is the bearer of genes.

chromosome number The usually constant number of chromosomes characteristic of a particular kind of animal or plant.

clone Two or more individuals with identical genetic material. Human clones occur naturally in the form of "identical twins." Though twins begin life with the same genetic material, they, nevertheless, develop distinct physical differences (fingerprints, for example). Furthermore, they become fully unique individuals with distinct personalities as a result of their different experiences and independent choices. An individual conceived by somatic cell nuclear transfer would be at least as different from his/her progenitor as natural twins.

coitus The physical union of male and female genitalia leading to the ejaculation of semen from the penis into the female reproductive tract; sexual intercourse.

cytoplasm All the contents of a cell, other than the nucleus. The cytoplasm is the site where many important processes occur, including the assembly of proteins and enzymes, and the manufacture of cell products. The cytoplasm also contains the mitochondria, small bodies that are responsible for the breakdown of food to produce the energy needed for the activities of the cell.

D & C Dilation (the action of stretching or enlarging an organ or part of the body) and curettage (a scraping). It refers to dilating the cervix and scraping the walls of the uterus to empty its contents.

D & X Dilation and extraction (sometimes called D & E [dilation and evacuation]) of a larger, more formed fetus that cannot just be scraped out as amorphous or nearly amorphous tissue.

diploid Denoting the state of a cell containing twice the normal gametic number of chromosomes, one member of each chromosome pair derived from the father and one from the mother; the normal chromosome complement of somatic cells.

DNA The molecular basis of heredity in many organisms. They are constructed of a double helix held together by hydrogen bonds between purine and pyrimidine bases that project inward from two chains containing alternate links of deoxyribose and phosphate.

embryo The early stages of development of a fertilized egg. In humans, the developing organism from conception until approximately the end of the second month or sometime in the third month. In somatic cell nuclear transfer, it refers to the early developmental stages of an enucleated egg after it has been fused with a somatic cell.

enucleated egg An egg cell from which the nucleus has been removed. This is usually accomplished by penetrating the cell with a fine glass needle and withdrawing the nucleus while observing under a microscope.

fetus An unborn vertebrate; a developing human being, usually from three months after conception.

gametes A mature germ cell capable of initiating formation of a new individual by fusion with another gamete. In heredity, any germ cell, whether ovum or spermatozoa.

gametocyte A cell that divides to produce gametes.

germ cell Reproductive cell. In mammals and humans, the germ cells are the sperm and eggs (ova).

gestation The period of time it takes an embryo to develop in the uterus, from a fertilized egg to a newborn offspring. Gestation begins with implantation of the embryo in the uterus and ends with birth.

insemination The deposit of seminal fluid within the vagina; normally introduced during intercourse, it can be accomplished by inserting a tube or catheter into the vagina in order to inject sperm.

in vitro ("in glass") Outside the living body and in an artificial environment. An egg may be fertilized outside the womb by implanting a sperm into the egg. When the two fuse and produce an embryo, the embryo can be transplanted into the uterus.

IVF In vitro fertilization.

nucleus The structure within a cell that contains the genetic material or genes. The nucleus is surrounded by a membrane that separates it from the remainder of the cell.

oocyte An egg before maturation, a female gametocyte.

ovum (plural, ova) An egg cell. A female reproductive cell.

partial-birth (late-term) abortion (The term *partial-birth abortion* does not appear in the medical dictionary.) Deliberate dilation of the cervix, usually over a sequence of days; instrumental or manual conversion of the fetus to a footling; breech extraction of the body except for the head; and partial evacuation of the intracranial contents of the living fetus to effect the vaginal delivery of a dead, but otherwise intact, fetus.

penis The organ of copulation in the male, formed of three columns of erectile tissue.

procreate To produce by the sexual act.

sentient Sensitive, capable of sensation.

somatic cell Any cell from the body of a mammal or human, other than the germ cells.

somatic cell nuclear transfer The technical name for the method used to produce the first animal clone, a sheep called "Dolly." The nucleus from a somatic cell is inserted into an enucleated egg. The nucleus from a somatic cell from another sheep was inserted into an enucleated egg that was then implanted into a yew for gestation.

sperm A male reproductive cell.

surrogate A person who functions in another's life as a substitute for some third person. Common usage in reproductive technology has reserved this designation for a woman who carries a pregnancy for a third person.

test-tube baby A lay term, not found in a medical dictionary. It refers to babies from eggs fertilized *in vitro*.

trimester A period of three months, one-third of the length of a human pregnancy.

ultrasound Vibrations of the same physical nature as sound but with frequencies above the range of human hearing. Ultrasound images, which look something like X-ray pictures, may be used to detect certain types of defects in fetuses.

urethra The urogenital canal leading from the bladder, discharging the urine externally. Female: a canal about 4 centimeters in length, passing from the bladder, in close relation with the anterior wall of the vagina. Male: a canal about 20 centimeters in length opening at the extremity of the glans penis; it gives passage to the spermatic fluid as well as the urine.

uterus The womb; the hollow muscular organ in which the impregnated ovum is developed into a child.

vagina The genital canal in the female, extending from the uterus to the vulva.

viability Capability of living; the state of being viable; usually connotes a fetus that has reached 500 grams in weight and twenty gestational weeks.

vulva The external genitalia of the female, the opening of the urethra and of the vagina.

zygote The diploid cell resulting from union of a sperm and an ovum. The individual that develops from a fertilized ovum.

INDEX

NAMES

SCRIPTURE

TOPICS